An Act Of
COMPASSION

FAYE P. BECKFORD

© Faye P. Beckford 2016

Copyright 2016

All rights reserved.

Bible references are taken from the King James Version, unless otherwise stated.

ISBN: 978-0-9937374-2-8

Faye P. Beckford
Scarborough, Ontario
innovision2u@yahoo.com

Ordering Information:

Special discounts are available on quantity purchases. For details, contact the publisher at the above email address.

The views and opinions expressed in this book are those of the author and do not necessarily reflect those of any organization named herein.

Dedication

To the memory of my dear mother, Iris Beckford, who, after listening to a speech I had written when I was ten years old, commented that some day, I would become a great lady. Well, I don't know about that—a mother can always dream. I'm still waiting. However, in my literary endeavors, her words have always remained in the back of my mind.

To the memory of my dear father, Arnold Beckford, who listened to the same speech and spoke no words, but gave his silent commendation by an approving smile. That memory has also remained with me.

Foreword

While at the checkout of a busy supermarket one afternoon, I noticed a counter with just a couple of people waiting in line. Thinking the cashier was about to close, I did not go to that counter. Instead, I joined the long queue. After a few minutes, the woman ahead of me turned and said, "I'd never go to *her* check-out; she is *so* unfriendly!" Others in the line agreed.

As I observed the young woman, I sensed something other than unfriendliness. Her facial expression seemed to suggest either physical pain, emotional trauma or a combination of both. True to my sensitive nature, I felt an urge to go to her checkout, so I could say hello and chat with her a bit. Yet, instead of acting on my instincts, I stood there, as if paralyzed, wondering how she might react.

I later regretted not having at least attempted to connect with the cashier. Although I have no way of knowing for sure, my guess is that a friendly interaction might have given her a lift, put a smile on her face and made her day--and mine!

It is an unfortunate fact that people seem more interested in receiving good feelings from others, than in conveying them to others. Human nature being what it is, we are more prone to take than we are to give, which is why, as the saying goes, "everyone loves a freebie".

Often, when people enquire about the well-being of others, they expect to receive a positive response. That makes the enquirer feel good. People, who, instead of engaging in the platitude of a polite reply, choose to give an honest answer, appear as complainers, whiners and social bores. As such, others often avoid them. It is not unusual to hear this expression: "Next time I see Mary, I'll just smile and wave, or say 'Hi' and walk quickly by". That might be the right approach, if you do not have the time or the interest in hearing what Mary has to say. Otherwise, she might just tell you exactly how she is doing or how she is feeling, annoying you and probably making you late for work!

Listening ears are like gold to hurting people.

What would be the point in asking Mary how she is doing, if you are going to blame her for telling you! That, however, is our conditioning. No one wants to be associated with gloom. Laugh, and the whole world laughs with you; cry and you cry alone, as the saying goes.

Generally, everyone wants to hear that everyone else is doing just fine, whether or not that is the case. Although it is beneficial to accentuate the positive, sometimes it is more beneficial to the psychological well- being of individuals to express what they are experiencing. However, no one wants to hear bad news, or to be around unhappy people.

We sometimes see the facial expression of others, not as a reflection of how *they* are feeling, but of how they feel about *us*. We give little or no consideration to the underlying emotions resulting in that expression, or how our interaction might help *them*. Often, our main concern is that *their* mood is not helping *us*. A world of difference could result from just one act or one word that says, "I care about what is happening with you. Your well-being matters to me".

This book shows the impact that a simple act of compassion could have on the life of a troubled individual. Here, a teenager reaches out to a classmate who was ostracized by everyone else in her class, because of her unfriendly appearance. Her intervention brought hope where there was despair and purpose where there was despondency in this unhappy teenager's family .Not only did this change the life of the rejected teenager and her family, but its impact also rippled out into the community, resulting in many other lives forever positively changed.

Table of Contents

Chapter 1	HEAVY STUFF	**1**
Chapter 2	WARM WELCOME	**25**
Chapter 3	FUN AND GAMES	**49**
Chapter 4	A NEW EXPERIENCE	**75**
Chapter 5	A STEP FORWARD	**112**
Chapter 6	A PERSISTENT KNOCK	**144**
Chapter 7	WHO IS THAT MAN?	**166**
Chapter 8	ALMOST UNREAL	**180**
Chapter 9	A REAL EYE-OPENER	**200**
Chapter 10	POINTS TO PONDER	**234**
Chapter 11	OLD THINGS	**245**
Chapter 12	THE LITTLE GROUP	**260**
Chapter 13	FAMILY REUNION	**289**
Chapter 14	ONWARD AND UPWARD	**300**

ONE

HEAVY STUFF!

Fair Crest High School stood amid a cluster of tall trees overlooking a lush, green, meticulously manicured lawn, flanked by a beautiful hedge of alternating flowerbeds and shrubs. Mrs. Burn's Tuesday morning classroom buzzed with excited chatter, as everyone recounted the events of a fun-filled summer.

The morning sun streamed in through the clear glass window and nestled softly on Kezia's desk, as she chatted happily with her friends. Suddenly the room became silent and all eyes turned, as a dejected young woman sauntered in and slumped heavily in her chair, pouting. She looked at no one and spoke to no one. That concerned Kezia.

"She looks so angry", Kezia whispered to Chantelle. "What's the matter with her?"

AN ACT OF COMPASSION

"How should I know?" Chantelle frowned.

"It might be a good idea to try talking to her. Maybe she'll tell us what's going on with her", Kezia suggested.

"You think so?" Chantelle responded, making no effort to conceal her lack of interest.

"I think she could probably use a friend", Kezia replied.

"You can talk to her, if you want to, but I won't. She's just a dud, if you ask me! She's so un-cool! "

"What if there's something wrong with her? What if she's sick, or something?" Kezia wondered aloud.

"Well, then, she should not be coming to school", Chantelle replied disdainfully. "There had better not be anything wrong with her. Like, I would *not* want to catch anything from her".

Just then, Mrs. Burns walked in. Silence followed. The concern, however, remained in Kezia's mind. She had a strong feeling she should try to interact with this girl. As soon as the bell sounded for the morning break, she went in search of her mysterious classmate, and found her sitting in a little corner of the cafeteria.

"What should I say to her?" Kezia pondered, as she sat at a table not too far away. Maintaining a safe distance, she observed the girl, hoping she would look her way. She thought a friendly smile might open the way for a conversation. That strategy did not work. She just sat there brooding over her strawberry smoothie and staring at the table. Kezia was ready with a smile for her, but she would not as much as look up.

Finally, Kezia decided to use the direct approach. If she did not act now, she would miss her chance. Break time would soon be over. Casting aside all apprehension, she summoned up her courage, got up and walked over to the table where the girl sat.

"Hi!" she said perkily, "May I sit down?"

Taken by surprise, the girl shot a quick, defiant glance at Kezia from across the table, and then looked quickly back down, without saying a word.

"I'm Kezia. My friends call me Kez".

The girl remained silent.

"It's kind of quiet here today", Kezia continued, trying to break the ice. With her eyes still fastened to the table, the girl shrugged indifferently.

"She shrugged!" Kezia thought, "At least that's something!"

Encouraged, Kezia ventured, "Mm, that looks good! I *love* strawberry smoothies. You barely touched yours though, and break's almost over!"

Still the girl made no reply.

"What's bothering you?" Kezia asked gently, but matter-of-factly. If she was going to get anywhere with this conversation, she thought, she had better get to the point.

"What do you mean what's bothering me?" the girl scowled, making eye contact for the first time, to Kezia's great surprise and delight. At least she was getting *some*where.

"It appears as if you have a lot on your mind!" Kezia replied. "You seem to be wor---

"How I seem is none of your business, okay! Just leave me alone!" the girl interrupted angrily.

"Don't be angry", Kezia responded delicately. "I

am not trying to pry".

"O no? You could have fooled me!" she retorted.

Just then, the bell rang, signaling the end of the morning break. The girl got up, tossed her unfinished smoothie in the garbage and stormed off, but not before throwing Kezia another defiant look.

Kezia caught up to her. "I know something's wrong; why don't you tell me? Maybe I can help", she persisted calmly.

"Help?" The girl laughed bitterly. "You think you can help? What do you think *you* can do?"

"I don't know", Kezia replied, a bit bewildered, and at a loss for words. "I don't know, but maybe…*something!* By the way, you didn't tell me your name?"

"No, I didn't!" she snapped.

"Would you mind telling me?" Kezia asked softly.

"Yes, I'd mind! Why should I tell you my name?"

"Well, for one thing, we're classmates! We might be working on the next science project together", Kezia smiled.

"If that happens, you'll find out then".

"Okay, let me guess!" Kezia persisted, holding her smile. "Hmm, let's see. Joyce? Candace? Natasha, maybe?"

"Okay! Okay! You're really annoying me. If you must know, my name is Marissa. Okay? Now buzz off!"

"Marissa! Cool name! Thank you for telling me. Okay, Marissa, something heavy seems to be going on with you. If you feel like talking about it at some time, I'm a good listener. I don't mean to be a bother. See you in class".

"Hope not. Good riddance!"

Ignoring the comment, Kezia turned and started jogging. She did not want to be late. Mrs. Burns might overlook a few seconds of lateness, but no one dared be late for Mrs. Draper's math class.

"Okay! You wanna know what's bothering me, you say? You think you can help?" Marissa blurted as Kezia took the first few steps.

"I can try!" Kezia stopped and turned, totally

surprised.

"Alright, then! Here's the deal. For starters, my parents are getting divorced, okay! What can *you* do about *that*? What can *anyone* do?"

"I'm *so* sor--", Kezia tried to empathize.

"Save it!" Marissa glared, as she sprinted off, leaving Kezia behind. This time there was no catching up to her.

Kezia reached her classroom, panting, only to find Mrs. Draper standing in front of the class with her face toward the blackboard, ready to begin. Trying hard to get to her seat without anyone noticing, she crept on tiptoes across the room, shoulders hunched, and quickly sat. She had forgotten that nothing escapes the eagle eyes of Mrs. Draper, one of which seemed to have been located conveniently at the back of her head.

"Kezia Lafontaine?" Mrs. Draper called, raising her eyes from her notes, just long enough to give a warning glance.

"O no! She *did* notice!" Kezia thought, embarrassed and a bit troubled. Thankfully, Mrs.

Draper was in a good mood. The warning glance was all she got. Her friend Chantelle, on the other hand, was not going to let her get off that easily.

"Where *were* you?" she hissed.

"I was talking to Marissa in the cafeteria", Kezia replied casually.

"Marissa? Who's that?"

"The girl we were talking about".

"So, *that's* her name!"

"Yeah".

"I looked all over for you, and you were there talking to *her*?"

"While you were in the washroom, I went to the cafeteria to find her. I should have told you I was going, so you wouldn't have to be searching for me, but I didn't have time to wait".

"I wanted to show you some pictures we took at the cottage over the weekend, but instead you went searching for *her*".

"Can I see them after school, maybe?"

"Maybe", Chantelle replied, disappointed.

"Silence everyone!" Mrs. Draper called, as she

completed writing on the blackboard.

During the math lesson, Kezia found it hard to concentrate. Her conversation with Marissa occupied her mind. After school, she again looked for Marissa, and found her at her locker.

"Why are you following me around?" Marissa demanded angrily.

"I couldn't get it off my mind. You know, what you told me earlier. I thought how much it must hurt—your parents getting divorced".

"Don't you have anything better to do than to stick your nose into other people's business?"

"I don't mean to do that, I just…"

"My dad's a drunk, okay! Satisfied?" Marissa blurted out angrily, unable to hold her emotion in check any longer. "That's why they're getting divorced! Okay! Is that what you wanted to know?"

"Oh! I'm so sorry, Marissa. That's really heavy stuff!"

"Look, I don't want your pity, okay!" Marissa replied defiantly. "Just leave me alone!"

Sensing Marissa's pain, Kezia, again ignored her

comment, and wondered what she could do to help. Looking at her contemplatively, as she strapped on her backpack, Kezia ventured:

"Marissa would you like to come to my house after school tomorrow?"

"What?" she asked incredulously, with her strap halfway up her arm.

"Would you like to come to my house?"

"Why would you want me to come to your house? You don't even know me", Marissa replied, as if confused, uncertain as to how she should react.

"That's true, I don't know you very well, but I'd like to be your friend, if you'd let me". Despite Marissa's defiance, Kezia was convinced that she could help in some way.

"Yeah, right! *You* want to be *my* friend".

"Yes, that's right". Kezia again replied matter-of-factly.

"You have lots of friends. Why would you want to be friends with *me*?"

"Will you at least think about coming?"

"There's nothing to think about. Just leave me alone!"

"All right, then. I will, if that's what you really want, but on one condition".

"What's that?"

"That you take my phone number in case you change your mind".

"You don't give up, do you?" Marissa replied somewhat subdued, as she hesitantly reached out to take the paper Kezia handed her. Though she would never admit it, Kezia's gentle, caring persistence was making an impression upon her that she could hardly conceal.

"Nope! I don't", Kezia smiled broadly, "so will you come?"

"You are something else!" Marissa said, shaking her head and gazing at Kezia, as if studying her. "Alright! I'll think about it, but I'm not promising anything!"

"Good enough!" Kezia replied optimistically, as she turned to start her journey home. "See ya tomorrow!" she called cheerily, heading for the

AN ACT OF COMPASSION

shortcut to her house.

As she stepped in the door, Cuddles her cat came to greet her. Bending down she swept him up into her arms, rustling his coat. "Hi, cutie!"

"Hi Kez!" her Mom called from the kitchen. Setting down Cuddles, she made her way to the kitchen.

"How was your day at school?" her Mom smiled.

"Quite interesting!" Kezia replied, embracing her Mom.

"I want to hear all about it, but first, you're not going to believe this. Your cousin Jordan called today. He's getting married!"

"Awesome! When's the wedding?" Kezia asked excitedly.

"It's in December. We should be receiving the formal invitation soon".

"Alright! We're going to Florida! I can't wait!" Kezia could not contain her excitement, but suddenly became serious. "Mom, there is something I need to tell you".

"What's that, love? I hope nothing's wrong", her

Mom responded, a bit uneasy.

"I invited one of my classmates home for dinner tomorrow evening. Sorry I didn't check with you first, but I really wanted to help her. Hope it's okay". She then told her Mom about Marissa, and the concern she felt for her.

"You did a very nice thing --inviting her home. It's *quite* okay", her Mom reassured her.

"I hope she'll come!" Kezia said eagerly.

"Oh, I think she will, but if she doesn't, don't be too disappointed. It takes time to build trust. We'll welcome her whenever she chooses to come". Kezia found those words very consoling.

"Thanks, Mom!" she smiled, "you're the best!"

Meanwhile, Marissa, on her way home, could not put out of her mind her encounter with Kezia, and the interest she had shown in her. Although the intrusion annoyed her, she knew that it was with good intention. She thought of how this girl had gone out of her way to be kind to her. She could not believe she wanted her to come to her house, and to be her friend! "Well, I doubt I'll go", she thought, "but I must admit, it feels *real* good to have been asked".

Marissa got home and found no one there. The absence of her Dad when she walked through the door was a treat. She had dreaded coming home and finding him drunk again. Not seeing him, she breathed a sigh of relief, unloaded her heavy backpack, washed her hands and put her TV dinner in the microwave, while she found her favorite channel. Soon dinner was ready.

Positioning herself comfortably in her favorite chair, she sat and watched cartoons, while she feasted on French fries and chicken nuggets. What bliss! She thought. However, it was not to last. Before she could finish her last mouthful, she heard the key turn in the lock.

"O No! He's home!" she thought, as she headed for the stairs in an attempt at hurrying to her room before he got in, but it was too late. Half-way up the stairs, she heard a voice behind her,

"Hi, Marissa!"

She turned abruptly

"O Mom! It's you! Hi! You're home early!" she exclaimed, greatly relieved. "Thank God!" she muttered under her breath, as she returned to her spot. Her Mom had worked irregular hours all week, and could really use a rest. She spoke with Marissa briefly and went to her room.

Shortly afterwards, she heard a knock at the door. Thinking it was a salesperson, she ignored it. Again the knock came. Looking out at the porch, she saw her Dad standing there. The dreaded moment had come. She could not escape now. He had seen her. She wondered why he was not using his key, but she had no choice. She had to open the door.

"Hi Dad!" she greeted him, mustering up a smile.

"What took you so long to open the door?" he growled. Passing by her, he went to the bathroom, and then to the kitchen to make coffee. Cup in hand, he went to the bedroom, where her mother was. That made her anxious, and with good reason. Within minutes, she could hear his raised voice. An argument had erupted. "Mom needs her sleep", she thought. "Why did he have to go and disturb her now?"

Her uneasiness grew, as the argument continued. It quickly escalated, and although she knew what was about to happen, she knew she was powerless to do anything about it. Before long, she could hear her mother's screams as the blows landed on her.

"Dad, stop! Stop!" she yelled repeatedly from the other side of the closed door, to no avail. She felt every blow as if it had connected with her own body. It did not last long, but it felt like forever. As soon as he left the room, she rushed in. "Mom, are you okay?"

Uncontrollable sobbing answered her question. Feeling her mother's shame and her pain, she sat beside her on the bed, with her arms around her, as the tears streamed down her face. She experienced such rage, she wanted to confront her Dad, but she knew that would not be wise. He would not hesitate to transfer his anger to her. Her contempt heightened as she walked past him, sitting in the living room, drinking his coffee and watching television, as if nothing had happened. She went to the kitchen, got her Mom a glass of water and remained with her for a while.

All this time, she really wanted to release her feelings, but had no outlet. She even thought of calling the police, but decided against it, as she had done many times before. It would only have made matters worse. Besides, she knew her Mom would never have approved. She wished she could get herself and her Mom out of this situation. She was fed up with it. Right now, she just wished she had someone in whom she could confide—someone who could give her some kind of support.

Retreating to her room, she threw herself across her bed in desperation, "I'm fed up with this! I just want it to end". She thought of calling Jessica, one of her swimming companions, but she did not want her problems going around the neighborhood. She wondered about her Mom, and wanted to return to console her, but she needed some consolation herself. She would not be of much help in her present state.

AN ACT OF COMPASSION

A flood of emotions overpowered her. She felt confused, angry, helpless, alone and scared all at once. Bewildered, she shuddered, as her eye caught sight of an object glistening on her dressing table.

"That could be the answer", she thought, the tears again streaming down her cheeks. "What good am I, anyway? Apart from being my Dad's punching bag, what is my purpose on this planet? I can't even help my Mom, but I'm always bearing her pain and mine".

With trembling hands, she reached for the pair of scissors she had left there earlier, after using them to turn her torn pair of jeans into cut-off shorts. Instantly, before her hand touched the scissors, a piece of paper sticking out of her diary distracted her. Without knowing why, she had taken it out of the pocket of her backpack and placed it there earlier. Still trembling, she picked up her diary instead of the scissors, took the paper out and just stared at it. Minutes passed. Finally, she returned to some sense of composure. Pensively, she tapped the paper to her chin, and then reached for the telephone.

"Well, the moment of truth has arrived", she said aloud. "That's much sooner than I thought". She snorted, blew her nose, dried her eyes and dialed. By this time, Kezia had settled down to do her homework, and was just about to repeat the science theory she had memorized. Jolted by the shrill ring of the telephone, she wondered whether she should answer it, or let the caller leave a message. Hesitantly, she picked it up, ready to ask the person to call back, unless it was one of her classmates calling to ask for help with a question.

"Hello?" she answered, thinking of a way to dismiss her caller politely.

"Hi… Kezia?" the halting voice sounded in her ears.

"Yeah?" Kezia replied questioningly, trying not to let on that she did not recognize the voice.

"I know you must be wondering who this is".

"Keisha, right?"

"No, it's not Keisha. Actually, it's Marissa".

Stunned, Kezia stared at the telephone. A brief

moment of silence followed before she spoke.

"Marissa! Hi! What a surprise! What's happening!" she exclaimed, thinking to herself, "I can't believe she really called. That's awesome!"

"I didn't think I'd be calling you so soon, or even at all. Hope you don't mind".

"No, no. I don't mind at all. It's great that you called. Is everything okay?"

"Yeah", Marissa answered unconvincingly.

"Are you sure?"

"Everything's fine".

"Okay, that's good".

Silence followed.

"Finished your homework?" Kezia enquired, trying to get a conversation going.

"Not really", she replied.

"You sound a bit on edge", Kezia observed. "I didn't mean to pressure you about coming to my place tomorrow. It's okay whatever you decide".

"Oh, no, that's not it at all! That's not why I called".

"Something's troubling you, though. I can tell".

"It's that obvious?"

"I can hear it in your voice".

Again, silence.

"You're right", Marissa finally admitted, trying hard to fight back the tears. "Something's troubling me. It's my Dad".

"What's wrong with your Dad?"

"I'm sorry. I shouldn't have called".

"Oh, no, I'm glad you did. As I told you, I'm a good listener. I'm here for you. What's happening with your Dad? Is he sick?"

"No, he's not sick--well not in the way you mean it. He got into another one of his flare-ups tonight".

"Another one of his flare-ups?"

Her voice quivering, Marissa got right to the point. "He came home drunk, and hit my Mom".

"Oh!" Kezia gasped, raising her hand to her mouth, her eyes popping. "Is she alright?"

"I guess. At least nothing got broken--this time!"

"Oh! No! It's that bad?"

"It's-- it's worse. That's not even the half of it".

"Oh, my! I don't know what to say".

"It's okay. I shouldn't be laying all this on you", Marissa replied somewhat remorsefully.

"Oh, don't worry about that. Remember I told you I wanted to help in whatever way I could?"

"Yes, I remember".

At this time, Marissa seemed to have forgotten all her earlier attempts at being tough.

"I don't know how I can help, but I will think of something. For starters, I'll pray for you", Kezia offered, recognizing prayer as her first line of defense in difficult situations for which she had no solution.

"Prayer might work for some people; I doubt it will work for me, but thanks anyway", Marissa replied sadly.

"God is not partial. He is willing to help anyone. Has your Dad ever tried getting help?"

"No. He doesn't think he needs it".

"I see", Kezia responded, at a loss for words.

"He would not even go to Al Anon. Mom has tried to get him to go, but he doesn't think he has a drinking problem. He's always saying he just had a few drinks, and that he is not drunk. He tells my Mom it's her fault that he hits her, and that she deserves it. That makes me *so* mad, I could scream. I just want it to be over. Sometimes I feel like running away".

Carefully, she avoided mentioning the other option she had considered earlier. She knew that the thought of suicide that had come into her mind, would have been too much to lay on Kezia. It scared her to think that she had entertained the idea.

"I can't even imagine what you must be feeling", Kezia replied.

"If only she knew!" Marissa thought.

"Has he ever hit *you*?" Kezia asked cautiously, as if she had read Marissa's mind.

"I can't count the number of times".

"Really!" Kezia exclaimed in disbelief.

"Yep!" Marissa responded, followed by a snort and then silence.

Finally, Kezia spoke, trying to console her. "I don't know yet what I can do to help. I hope you'll come tomorrow. It will at least take your mind off things a bit. I can imagine it must be very difficult for you at home, but I'm glad you didn't run away tonight. That might have been even worse".

"You're right. That was a dumb idea".

"Did you have a good relationship with your Dad before he started drinking?"

"Oh yeah, before all this, I had a real cool Dad. Now, it's like I don't even know him".

Kezia reflected in silence for a while and then offered, "I don't know, but maybe my Dad could help your Dad".

"I don't think it would be a good idea to say anything to your Dad. I probably shouldn't have called".

"I won't say anything if you don't want me to, but call me anytime. Don't hesitate".

"Okay. Thanks. What time should I come tomorrow?"

"Awesome! I'm so glad you're coming! Dinner's at 5:30, but we could walk home together after school, if you'd like".

"That sounds great! See you tomorrow".

TWO

WARM WELCOME

Kezia tried to smile in her usual manner, as she walked into the classroom the following morning, but at the back of her mind was her concern for Marissa.

"Hey, Chantelle! How's it going?" she asked perkily, trying to mask her concern.

"Everything's cool. You sure left in a hurry yesterday!"

"Yeah, I wanted to catch up with Marissa".

"Who's Marissa?"

"You know, the girl I went to the cafeteria to see yesterday".

"Oh, *her* again. You never told me what you two talked about yesterday".

"No, I didn't, but, actually, I have something to tell you now".

"Oh, what's that?"

"You'll never believe this".

"What? Tell, tell!" Chantelle leaned her ears close, hoping to hear some exciting news.

"I invited Marissa to my place after school and she's coming. I know she's not your favorite person, but it would be great if you would come too".

"That's what you wanted to tell me? You invited *her* to your *house*? Are you *c-razy*? Is she your friend now? You don't even *know* her! What were you *think*ing?"

"You're right. I don't know her very well, but I don't think she's a murderer or an arsonist or a thief or anything like that".

"I wouldn't be too sure. She's so weird!"

"Yeah, yeah. She's *so-o* weird. Her name is really Lizzy, not Marissa. You know, Lizzy Borden, the axe murderer! So, I'll just ask my Dad to install a metal detector with a camera or something to spy out the axe she's hiding in her backpack, before she *ever* comes into our house. Then we'll search her thoroughly and take away all her weapons. That way we'll be safe. That should do it, don't you think?"

"Very funny! You can joke about it all you want, but I would not trust her. What do you want with her, anyway? She's totally un-cool! Look at the way she even dresses! She's so *yes*terday!"

"Oh, c'mon Chantelle. She's just a girl like us. She could use a friend like anybody else. However strange you may think she is, she has feelings and needs just like the rest of us. I'd like to help her. Try and be nice to her".

"What do you mean you'd like to help her? Help her how?"

"She's going through a real rough time, and she needs someone to lean on".

"That's not gonna be me. You can try to get to know more about her if you want, but I don't know, and I don't care. I don't like her. She does not belong in our group. She's just a dud".

"It would be real nice if you would come to my place after school. We might not have as much fun as when we hang out with our other friends, but you never know".

"You must be joking. I can't even *imagine* an evening in *her* company".

"If you get to know her you might change your mind about her. She might be real nice after all. Who knows? She could probably be a lot of fun to be around if she loosens up".

"I told you. I *don't* like her. I don't want anything to do with her".

"It's hard to know whether or not you like someone, when you don't know anything about them, but if you would rather not come, it's up to you. You know you're always welcome, if you change your mind".

"I know enough to know I don't wanna be seen with her. You can be her friend if you like, but as I said, she does not belong in our group. As a matter of fact, you are either her friend or mine!"

"I can't believe you just said that".

"It's like this. Nobody talks to her. If you are her friend, nobody will talk to you. If I'm *your* friend, nobody will talk to *me*. It's that simple". Chantelle clarified her position.

For the rest of the day, Chantelle spoke not a word to Kezia, and ignored every attempt of Kezia's to interact with her. Kezia finally decided she would give her space, hoping that with time, things would work themselves out. In the meantime, she continued to reach out to Marissa. Her decision was firm, whatever Chantelle decided.

After school, Kezia and Marissa walked the four blocks to her house. Although they did not talk very much on the way, Marissa felt less anxious about her situation, and much more comfortable with Kezia than before. She reflected on the events of the previous night and felt a deep sense of appreciation that Kezia had taken the time to listen to her problem. She felt safe confiding in Kezia, and sensed a bond developing between them. She liked that feeling.

They arrived to the smell of a delicious aroma coming from the kitchen, where Kezia's Mom was busy preparing dinner. True to her hospitable nature, she had a fruit and cheese platter and a warm welcome waiting for her daughter and her guest.

AN ACT OF COMPASSION

"Hi, Kez!" she smiled, as they greeted each other with a loving embrace. "How was your day?"

"I had a great day, Mom. How was yours?"

"My day was wonderful! Do you remember that new assistant I hired?"

"You mean Esther?"

"Yes. She is lightening my workload tremendously. I left earlier than usual today, so I could get a head start on dinner".

"I can tell by that great smell", Kezia said excitedly, savoring the aroma of her favorite dinner rolls.

"Oh, can you?" Her Mom smiled.

"Oh, yeah! You can smell those rolls from the street. They smell heavenly!"

"Hope they'll taste as good", her Mom replied modestly.

"You know they will. You make the best rolls in town!"

"Why, thank you! With that commendation, I think I might enter the baking contest at the Farmer's Fair next year", her Mom replied jokingly.

"I think you should! No kidding!"

"I'll keep that in mind. Now, are you going to introduce me to your friend?"

"Oh, I'm sorry!" Placing a hand on Marissa's shoulder, she said. "Mom, this is my classmate, Marissa McBride. Marissa, my Mom, Leah Lafontaine".

"Hi, Marissa! It's so nice to meet you! Welcome to our home", Kezia's Mom smiled warmly, as she embraced Marissa.

"Nice meeting you, too, Mrs. Lafontaine", Marissa returned, pleasantly surprised that instead of a handshake, she had received an embrace. She found that very comforting.

"Pardon us for yapping away like that", Kezia's Mom apologized.

"That's okay". Marissa smiled shyly. "If only I could yap away with my Mom like that!" she thought. "Mom's okay, but we hardly have any time together; she has to work so hard".

"Thank you for coming. Please make yourself at home", Mrs. Lafontaine offered cordially.

"Thank you", she replied, looking around at the pictures on the wall of the beautiful, impeccably kept house. A feeling of warmth and tranquility had swept over her the moment she entered. She now felt very secure in the company of Kezia and her Mom.

"Come with me to the den", Kezia invited her, leading the way. "Do you like fish?"

"Oh, yeah! I *love* them!" Marissa smiled excitedly.

"Great! We just got a new aquarium with all kinds of awesome ones. Let's go see them".

"Cool!" Marissa replied eagerly.

"It's time for their feeding too! Can't keep them waiting!" Kezia smiled, making her way down the stairs.

"Having an aquarium with lots of fish must be tons of fun!" Marissa exclaimed.

"It is", Kezia agreed. "I especially like to watch them eat".

Marissa gasped in awe as they entered the den and she saw the huge aquarium, which almost stretched across a whole wall, with all kinds and sizes of fish of every color, swimming around in the clearest blue water she had ever seen.

"Wow! That's awesome!" She exclaimed.

"Yeah, it's pretty cool!" Kezia agreed, with pride. It was her responsibility to care for the aquarium and she did it expertly. As she poured the food in, the aquarium came alive with the incessant moving of fish snatching at bits of food as they floated down the tank.

The two watched in sheer amazement as dormant ones awoke and rushed to the feed, grabbing, snipping, slithering and flapping their fins. It was a beauty to behold. For a moment, the peace and tranquility of this scenery caused Marissa to escape her own reality and enter into another world.

Watching fascinated as the fish frolicked about, Marissa reflected on the closeness she sensed between Kezia and her Mom. She admired that. She almost envied it.

"Your Mom's so cool!" she said to Kezia.

"Oh yeah, she's *way* cool", Kezia agreed, smiling contentedly.

For a brief moment, Marissa again entered into dreamland, trying to picture her family being like Kezia's.

"What you're trying to do is real nice", she said."I mean, going out of your way to help me and all?" But in her heart, she held out no hope for a solution to her problem. She saw no way of ever again having a happy home. Kezia, noticing the sudden shift in her expression, guessed what she was thinking.

"I believe that God can do all things", she said, trying to offer the best consolation she could. "He can help your family".

"What I told you was just a part of it. I don't know if anyone can do anything to fix our situation".

"There's nothing too hard for the Lord", Kezia reassured her.

"Do you think He could save our house, *and* change my Dad *and* keep us together? Can He do all of that?"

"God can do all things; but what do you mean can he save your house?"

"Mom says we might lose our house", Marissa replied sadly.

"Oh no!" Kezia gasped.

"Yep, I could be homeless soon. Well, maybe not homeless. We'd have to get an apartment or something. Dad lost his job and Mom says she won't be able to pay the mortgage all by herself, but when my parents split, they'll have to sell the house anyway, so…"

Losing your home and having your family shattered all at once! How frightening that must be, Kezia thought. She thanked God for her parents and for the security that she felt within her own family. She had a kind, gentle and caring father and a sweet loving mother. They were always there for her. She knew she could depend on them.

Her Dad even helped with her homework at times, especially math and science. She could not imagine life without him coming home every day. She felt deep sympathy for Marissa. Not only did she not have a close relationship with her father, she was afraid of him. "Dear Lord, please help Marissa and her family", she prayed inwardly.

"Kezia, what's your Dad like?" Marissa broke the silence, as if reading her thoughts.

"He's *totally* cool! *Totally!*" Kezia beamed. "He'll be home any minute now. You'll soon get to meet him... Ah! Here he comes now!" She exclaimed excitedly at the sound of the doorbell. Rushing to the door, she wrapped her slender arms around his sturdy frame.

"Hi, sweetheart!" he smiled, as he bent to kiss her. "How was your day?"

"I had a great day, Dad. How was yours?"

"Pretty exciting, actually! I'll tell you all about it later". Glancing toward Marissa with a smile, he asked, "Who do we have here?"

"Dad, this is my friend, Marissa, from school. Marissa, this is my Dad, Dr. David Lafontaine", Kezia smiled, again placing her hand on Marissa's shoulder.

"Very nice to meet you, Marissa!" he smiled warmly, shaking her hand.

"Nice meeting you too, Dr. Lafontaine", Marissa

returned, beginning to feel even more relaxed, hearing Kezia refer to her as her friend, and feeling the warmth and caring conveyed by her touch.

"Dad, Marissa's having dinner with us", Kezia announced.

"Wonderful! Nice having you, Marissa. Welcome to our home", he said, with the warmest smile.

"Thank you", Marissa returned.

"See you two at dinner", he said, as he walked toward the kitchen to greet his wife.

"Hi, honey! How was your day?" he asked, bending to kiss her upturned cheek.

"I had a great day, dear. How was yours?" she smiled, as she turned from the kitchen sink, releasing the handful of leafy vegetables she was preparing, and drying her hands on her apron.

"My day went really well. My team had to deal with a very difficult situation today, but God gave us a miracle. I'm really happy with the way things turned out."

"That's wonderful! It seems to have been very

stressful. You look a bit drained".

"Yeah, it was actually *quite* stressful, I must admit".

"Would you like to talk about it?"

"We operated on a man who fell from the roof while working on a house. He suffered massive head injury. It didn't seem likely that he would have made it through the surgery, but God came to our help. We worked for hours, but it was all worth it in the end. Needless to say, he'll be away from housetops for quite some time, but otherwise, he's going to be just fine".

"Oh, that's a great ending! Does he have a family?"

"Oh, yeah! Young fellow 35 years old with a wife and 7 year old daughter, and a baby on the way".

"Thank God he's going to be alright".

"Yes, God be praised", Dr. La Fontaine was always careful to give God credit for every successful operation he performed. He was always mindful that healing comes only from God, and prayed for guidance before undertaking any procedure.

"Now, it's my turn to give you some good news. David, would you believe that that rosebush we were thinking about cutting down actually bloomed! I noticed it this morning as I was watering the garden. It has quite a few buds on it!"

"You're kidding! Really?"

"See for yourself!" she said, leading him to the window.

"Well, what d'you know! Soon we'll have lots of fresh roses!"

"We sure will!"

"Oh, that reminds me", he said, as he walked to the entrance table, returning with his hands behind his back, a sign she recognized well.

"David La Fontaine, you didn't", she smiled in anticipation.

"Ta d-a-a-h!" Bringing out from behind him the loveliest bouquet of flowers, he handed them to her.

"Oh! Roses! My favorite! Thank you!" she exclaimed, as she sniffed the delicate fragrance, letting out a sigh of sheer pleasure. "There's nothing like the smell of fresh roses".

Taking them back with her to the living room, she found the perfect spot on the dinner table for them, where they blended right in with the décor. Hurrying back to the kitchen, she found him standing by the counter.

"Thank you!" she glowed, planting a kiss on his cheek. "They are beautiful! If I didn't know you better, I'd ask what's the occasion".

"You're right. You *do* know me better. The only occasion I need for bringing flowers is coming home to you".

"Aw! That's so sweet! I always like when you surprise me, especially with roses. They smell wonderful!"

"Speaking of smell, that aroma is making me hungry. There's just something about the smell of cilantro that opens up my appetite", he said, as he checked out the salad dressing his wife was whipping up.

"Well, you'll soon be able to satisfy that perked-up appetite of yours. Dinner is almost ready. Kez, would you give me a hand, please?" She called, jolting her and Marissa out of their aquatic wonderland.

"I'll be there in a moment, Mom". Kezia replied, as she made her way to the bathroom to wash her hands. Marissa, before long, returned her attention to the aquarium, enjoying the feeling of calm that it gave to her.

"Would you put the salad on the table for me, please, honey?" her Mom requested as she entered the kitchen.

"Sure Mom! Mm, something smells *real* good!"

"Hope your friend will like this meal", Leah said. "I am aware that it might not make the average teenager jump for joy".

"I'm sure she'll enjoy it".

Soon the beautifully set table boasted an array of delectable dishes. A combination of an attractive bouquet from the flower garden, blended with Leah's roses, formed the centerpiece. It made for a lovely presentation that would arouse any appetite.

AN ACT OF COMPASSION

The elegant, yet modestly decorated table and dining room reflected the warmth and hospitality for which Leah La Fontaine was known. She could have made her home elaborate if she wanted, but she preferred it to be welcoming to her guests from all walks of life.

"Soup's on!" she called, as she brought in the last dish. Without hesitation, everyone gathered at the table. Her husband gave thanks to God for His provision, and asked His blessings upon the meal and upon all who would partake of it.

Dinner consisted of a luscious green salad, Leah's famous rolls, delectable steamed vegetables, brown rice, and a mouth-watering home-made "chicken" dish.

"This meal is delicious!" Marissa commented as she started on the main course. "I especially like the chicken!"

"Thank you", Leah responded, happy that Marissa was enjoying the meal, "but I must tell you, the only thing chicken about this dish is the seasoning. It's prepared the same as chicken, but it's all vegetable protein".

"It's all vegetables?" Marissa asked, as if shocked.

"Yes, it's protein that comes from plant sources alone", Leah replied, not at all surprised at her reaction.

"Wow! That's amazing! You could never tell".

"Marissa is right, Mom. This "vege-chicken" is excellent! But the rolls are still my favorite", Kezia smiled, as she reached for another. "What do you think, Marissa?"

"Yeah, they are totally awesome!" Marissa agreed.

"Thank you", Leah smiled.

"So, Mrs. La Fontaine, your family eats only what comes from plants?" Marissa asked.

"Yes, that's right", Leah smiled.

"Kezia, is that why you don't eat lunch at the cafeteria?"

"Yes, mainly that's the reason. It would be nice if they sold even vegetarian hamburgers, but they don't, so I prefer to take my own lunch to school".

AN ACT OF COMPASSION

"I see. I'm just curious: Is there something wrong with eating meat, Dr. Lafontaine?" Marissa wanted to know.

"Not really. God allows consumption of certain animals, but the diet He originally gave to human beings, comprised of things that grew directly from the ground. We believe it is healthier to follow God's original diet, and avoid eating meat altogether, if possible", he replied.

"That's very interesting. I have always thought of vegetarians as strange people who protect cows, and cheat rabbits out of their food!" Marissa ventured, at which the table exploded with laughter.

"What I mean is, I have always thought that vegetarians ate only lettuce and carrots and things like that", she explained, as the laughter subsided.

"Lettuce and carrots are very healthy, and we eat a lot of those, but in order to achieve and maintain optimal health, our bodies require a good balance of all the essential nutrients. That means making sure to include all the food groups. In our family, we get all our nutrients from plant sources. We also believe it is important to exercise, drink plenty of water and put our trust in God, rather than to lean on our own understanding, because He is the giver and the preserver of life and health", Kezia's Mom explained.

"I see", Marissa replied, nodding contemplatively.

"Now you can say you have met real live vegetarians, and they don't live out in the wilderness somewhere, nibbling on carrots and weeds and-- except maybe for this one—they're not the least bit strange!" Kezia quipped.

"No, they're not at all strange", Marissa smiled.

"I must add, though, that being total vegetarian might not be possible for everyone. It is not wrong to eat animal protein, if you have to, as long as you eat the right kinds in the right quantity, prepared in the right way. God gives us instructions in His word as to what kind of animal protein is good for food, and which is not. If you are familiar with the Bible and are interested in knowing more, you can read about it in Leviticus 11", Dr. Lafontaine offered.

AN ACT OF COMPASSION

"Okay. Thank you", Marissa responded, surprised that the Bible gives such information.

"Dad, do you think that people will eat meat in heaven?" Kezia asked.

"I really don't think so", he replied.

"I don't either", Kezia said. "I can't imagine someone in heaven chasing a chicken when it's time to prepare dinner".

"That's true; all of God's creatures will be safe there", her Dad responded.

"I think that our diet will return to the original one that God gave to Adam and Eve in the beginning. Those who are not able to follow a total plant based diet now will have no difficulty doing so in the earth made new", Kezia's Mom commented. "Everyone will be able to enjoy the wonderful things in store for all who will inhabit the Promised Land".

"You're so right", Dr. Lafontaine agreed.

Dinner ended with homemade apple pie and herbal tea, consisting of an aromatic blend of fruit and ginger. After dinner, Marissa offered to help with the cleaning up. Usually that's not her favorite thing to do, she confessed, but she felt more energetic than she usually did after a meal. She actually enjoyed helping. The kitchen now sparkling clean, the two went to Kezia's room to do their homework.

"You know, Marissa, I think it would be a good idea to tell someone, an adult maybe, what's happening with you at home. Even our guidance counselor might be able to help".

"My parents would not be happy about that. Mom does not want anyone knowing what is happening with her. That might make things worse. My Dad certainly doesn't want anyone knowing".

"I understand, but there must be someone who could help if they knew", Kezia replied. "I know you would prefer if I didn't say anything, but maybe my Mom and Dad could help, if they knew what was happening with your family".

"Mm, I don't know, Kezia. My parents like to keep family things private".

"When family things cause hurt it is sometimes necessary to bring them out into the open in order to find solutions. Anyway, I'll keep praying for you and your family, I am sure that God has the answer. He can change any situation. I want to help, but I don't know how. I pray that He will show me what I can do".

"You're already helping--a lot! Inviting me to your home was the nicest thing anyone could ever have done for me. Your listening to me last night did wonders for me. You have no idea! You have already been a great help".

"That's good to know. At least, it's a start".

THREE

FUN AND GAMES

Girl talk and homework now ended, the two joined Kezia's parents in the den, where they sat watching a documentary on television.

"Scrabble, anyone?" Kezia asked as soon as the documentary ended. "Marissa, do you play Scrabble?"

"I *love* Scrabble!" Marissa perked up "It's my favorite board game!"

"Oh, cool! Most of my friends find it boring. It's great to find someone my age who also likes playing!" Kezia smiled.

"I don't see how anyone could find Scrabble boring. It's so much fun!" Marissa responded excitedly.

"Are you a good player?" Kezia asked, trying to

feel out the competition.

"I think so. My sister dreaded playing with me when she was living at home. I used to give her a good whipping every time!" Marissa bragged.

"I see-ee!" Kezia said, mischievously. "You delighted in giving your sister a good letter whipping, huh? Well, you be prepared for one this time, 'cause you're getting it from me!"

"Oh, yeah?" Marissa took up the challenge. "We'll see about that!"

"Alright then! Game's on!" Kezia announced enthusiastically. "Mom, Dad, are you in?"

"We sure are! Right, honey?" Her Mom prodded.

"Right, right", her Dad answered, with pretended enthusiasm.

You see, Kezia's Dad had won the last match by a whopping ten points! Now, that just is not done! Leah Lafontaine was the Scrabble queen, and nobody beats her and lives to brag about it! She was going to get him good this time, and he knew it!

"Are you prepared, Dad? You know what you're in for, don't you?" Kezia teased.

"Are you ladies planning to gang up on me again?" her Dad asked good-humoredly.

"You know it!" Kezia grinned.

He knew that the competition was going to be hot. His desire to hold on to the coveted crown was equal to his wife's eagerness to reclaim it. As the four positioned themselves around the table, ready to go, Kezia whispered to Marissa, "It's a grudge match".

"Really?" Marissa whispered back.

"Yeah", Kezia replied, followed by giggles.

"What are you two whispering and giggling about?" Kezia's Dad nudged her jokingly, as they drew their letters. "Planning your strategy, are you?"

The two responded with more giggles.

Although neither Marissa nor Kezia had played for a while, they played like pros. It did not take them long to nail the double and triple letter scores. Marissa's problems took a backseat to the fun of the game and the ambiance of the Lafontaine household. At least for a few hours, this dour girl had been transformed into a cheerful, happy teenager. Kezia wondered silently at the amazing difference in her personality compared to when they had first met. She was actually a lot of fun!

As Kezia's turn came around and everyone waited for her to make her move, her Dad made conversation with Marissa.

"Do you live around here, Marissa?"

"Yes, I do. I live on Spring Blossom Drive".

"Oh, we're neighbors, then. That's just down the road from us!"

"Yes, it's just a few blocks away", Marissa smiled.

"Have you lived there long?"

"I grew up there", Marissa replied with a sense of pride.

"Oh, did you?" he smiled.

"Yes. You probably noticed that back yard with the tree house?"

"It's an eye-catcher. Is that your house?"

"Yes. My parents made it for my sister and me when we were little", Marissa answered pensively, reflecting on the good days of the past.

"It's very creative. Are your parents in the design business or something like that?"

"No. Actually, my mother is a nurse. My Dad used to be an ambulance driver".

"Used to be?"

"Yes. He's not working now", Marissa volunteered, not being sure why. Usually, she would not give that information out, but she felt very relaxed in the company of this family.

"No?" he responded, thinking it unlikely that Marissa's Dad could be retired, but not wanting to pry.

Sensing his curiosity, she replied impulsively, "He got let go from his job".

"I'm sorry. That must be very hard on your family", he replied empathetically.

As Kezia finished her move, she heard her Dad's comment, to which she responded:

"You're right, Dad. Alcohol addiction must be a very difficult thing to deal with".

"Alcohol addiction?" he asked aghast.

At that, Marissa shot a bewildered glance at

Kezia, and then lowered her eyes to the floor.

"Oh, I'm so sorry, Marissa, I thought you...I thought you had--" Kezia tried awkwardly to explain. She thought Marissa had told her father about the addiction problem her family was experiencing, and by that assumption, had inadvertently revealed Marissa's secret.

"It's okay, Kez. Don't worry about it. Maybe it's better that it came out this way", Marissa consoled her, while trying to conceal her own embarrassment.

"Marissa, I am so very sorry!" Dr. Lafontaine's heart went out to her.

"What your family must be going through!" his wife, Leah added. The game stopped for a moment, as the family contemplated Marissa's situation.

"Yes, it's very hard", Marissa admitted, her eyes fastened to the floor. To her surprise, instead of being angry with Kezia for blurting out her problem, she felt a great sense of relief, knowing that others shared her pain. Returning their concentration to the game took some effort, as Marissa's problem weighed heavily on the minds of everyone.

A FUN-FILLED EVENING

"Let's take a break", Leah suggested Kezia's Dad then offered to have a word of prayer for Marissa and her family. That was a new experience for Marissa. Praying was not a part of her family's lifestyle, but it gave her an unexpected sense of security and comfort. After the prayer, Leah headed for the kitchen, returning shortly afterwards with juice and oatmeal cookies.

Refreshed and encouraged, everyone returned to the game with a new fervor. Kezia had invited Marissa home, with the intention that the change of atmosphere might relieve her stress, even if only for a brief moment. She would not let go of that goal. She was determined to do all she could to make it a fun-filled evening for Marissa.

With her special brand of humor, that would not be very difficult. When her turn came around to make a word, she spotted a vacant space for a triple word score that would accommodate a word ending with the letter "E". Grinning with mischief in her eyes, she joined three of her letters to that vacant "E", to the sheer astonishment of her Dad.

"That's *not* a word!" he protested.

"Yes it is!" she replied, straight-faced.

"Not in the English language it isn't!"

"Yes it is!"

"Vife" is *not* a word", he insisted.

"Yes, it is!" Kezia stood her ground.

"There is *no* such word!" her Mom agreed enthusiastically.

"Sure there is!" Kezia asserted, trying hard to maintain her straight face.

"*Vife*? That is *not* a word!" her Mom repeated.

"It is *so*!" Kezia continued. "I can prove it!"

"Okay, go ahead! Prove it!" her Dad challenged.

"This I have to see", her Mom said eagerly, amused.

"Okay! I will! I'll prove it".

"We're waiting!" her parents chorused.

"Find it for us in the dictionary", her Dad added.

"I have better proof than the dictionary".

"Oh, do you really?" her Mom responded, even more amused.

"Yes, Mr. Ishban, our chemistry teacher brought

his vife to our classroom last Wednesday".

"His *vife*?" her Dad frowned.

"Yes, his vife!" Kezia repeated.

"Okay, go on! Describe that for us", he urged.

"Well, she's very pretty. She's a lawyer! She---"

"Grab her!" he commanded, as she got up to run, knowing what she had coming to her. Now, despite all her efforts, she was powerless to contain the laughter, as it broke forcefully through her tightly pressed lips.

"Leah, sponge bats or cushions?" he asked with an eager grin.

"Sponge bats, definitely!" she answered, equally eager. "Marissa, here's yours".

For the next few moments, mock screams and laughter filled the room, as the three took out their fury on Kezia, bringing down their sponge bats upon her in alternating sequence from every angle.

"Okay, okay!" she pleaded, amid spurts of laughter, as the bats landed incessantly upon her. "I've learned my lesson! I've learned my lesson! Mercy, please!"

AN ACT OF COMPASSION

"Mercy, you say? What did you learn?" her Dad demanded, his face reddened from the laughter and the vigorous exercise.

"I learned that your vife has very strong arms", Kezia continued mischievously, laughing more heartily as she again tried to escape.

"That one deserves a cushion! Leave her to me!" her Mom grinned, as she reached for her favorite down-filled square cushion.

"I'll help!" Marissa joined in with her sponge bat.

"What did you learn?" he repeated.

"I learned that your vife is a fast runner".

"I see. The lesson hasn't quite sunk in", he said, as he brought down his bat another time.

For the next few minutes the avalanche of sponge bats and cushion continued left, right and center on Kezia.

"Okay, okay! Really, I've learned my lesson now". Her laughter subsided, reduced to a broad smile.

"What did you learn?" he repeated.

"I have learned that I love you guys and that its time to get back to the game and make a real word. Deal?"

"Not yet!" he grinned. "Who did Mr. Ishban bring to your class last Wednesday?"

"He brought his v---ouch!" She grimaced in mock pain as her Dad's sponge bat came down yet again on her head.

"Who did Mr. Ishban bring to your class last Wednesday?"

"Okay, Dad, Mr. Ishban brought his wife to our class last Wednesday", she panted.

"That's better! *Now* we have a deal".

"Good! I'm exhausted", her Mom agreed, as she brought down her cushion on Kezia's head one last time, and then flopped on to the couch, panting, joined by her husband and Marissa.

"I have never had so much fun!" Marissa declared, trying to catch her breath.

"Just leave it to Kez to brighten up a game!" her Mom agreed.

"Seriously, though, Kez, I hope you kids are not

AN ACT OF COMPASSION

making fun of Mr. Ishban", her Dad said.

"Oh! No! We love him *and* his vife".

"Kezia Lafontaine?" her Mom cautioned, narrowing her smiling eyes. "Our weapons are still at arm's length!"

"Okay. Got it Mom. Let's get back to the game. I promise I'll behave. We never make fun of Mr. Ishban; he's a very good teacher and a very nice man".

"That's good to know", her Dad smiled.

Kezia's antics had certainly lifted the spirits of everyone, but should she continue, they would not have been able to finish the game, so, hard as it was, she kept her promise that she would behave. On Scrabble nights, the Lafontaines reserve the right to pummel with sponge bats anyone who deliberately made a non- existent word. Kezia got the bats every time!

The game ended with the former deposed Scrabble queen reclaiming her crown. She had settled the score, and regained her bragging rights, but her husband was not about to concede defeat that easily. He challenged her to the next game.

"I am yielding it for now, but I will r-r-rise again!" He announced, raising his right index finger, trying to sound very regal, as he took off the gold-covered-cardboard crown from his head, and placed it on his wife's. Stepping back, he saluted the queen, who tilted her crown in response. So comical was that scene, it cracked up everyone, even the queen!

"Don't be too sure of reclaiming that crown, Dad. *I* might be wearing it next time around". Kezia warned.

Scrabble was the favorite board game of the Lafontaine family, and their most enjoyable indoor recreational activity. Win or lose, everyone hugely enjoyed the game and the time spent together.

As all good things must end, or so the saying goes, the time had come to call it quits to an exhilarating, fun-filled evening. For a few hours, Marissa had left her cares behind, and immersed herself in the nurturing environment of the Lafontaines. Ending the evening brought a bit of sadness to her, but she knew she would carry the memory of this experience with her for a long time to come.

"Thanks again for inviting me to your home, Kezia. I had an awesome time", Marissa smiled, as she picked up her backpack.

"I am glad you came, Marissa", Kezia replied. "I really enjoyed your company".

"Thank you for having me, Dr. and Mrs. Lafontaine. It was great spending the evening with your family".

"It was a pleasure having you, Marissa", Leah responded.

"Yes it was", her husband agreed. "Come again".

"Thank you", Marissa smiled.

"How cool are these people!" she thought on the way to the car.

After a few minutes in their comfortably cushioned blue Mercedes, the Lafontaines pulled into the McBride driveway. Marissa thanked them again, and waved good-bye, as she stepped into the doorway of her house.

"Bye, Marissa!" Kezia called from the back seat.

A FUN-FILLED EVENING

"See you tomorrow!"

"Yes, tomorrow morning bright and early!" Marissa replied, and with a satisfied smile, she entered her house.

"Hi Mom!" she bubbled, as she walked into the living room, where her Mom sat leisurely perusing the pages of a professional periodical, as she waited for her to come home.

"Hi, 'Marissa, how was your evening?"

"It was awesome!"

"That's good. By any chance, did you get home on a hot air balloon or something?"

"What do you mean?"

"You seem to be on top of the world!"

"Oh, yeah! I'm feeling pretty good. I had a great time tonight at Kezia's".

"That's good! Would you like to tell me about it?"

"Sure! For starters, Kezia and I hung out together and had a good talk. By the way, she has the coolest aquarium ever! I had a great time watching the most awesome fish. Then I had a vegetarian dinner out of

AN ACT OF COMPASSION

this world, and a great dessert with herbal tea. For the rest of the evening we played Scrabble. It was *so* much fun".

"Oh, joy", her Mom responded in the most apathetic tone she could muster. "You spent time with some fish, ate rabbit food and played a game of Scrabble! *So* much fun!" she teased.

"I know it doesn't sound like it, Mom, but it really *was* a lot of fun". Marissa could never gain her mother's interest in playing Scrabble.

"Ho hum!" she continued, faking a yawn, which looked as funny as she intended it, getting a burst of laughter from Marissa.

"I know Scrabble is not your favorite game, but even you would have enjoyed it, believe me. This one was different".

"Good thing I wasn't there. You and your Dad are the only two people who know that I snore and I'd like to keep it that way".

"You would not even get as far as closing your eyes, much less to snore. Any expression of boredom would be nothing that a sponge bat or two would not swiftly cure".

"Sponge bats? What are you talking about?"

"Oh, you had to have been there. Anyway, how was *your* evening, Mom?"

"It was pretty good. I caught up on some things I had to do, since I had the evening all to myself. Seriously though, Marissa, I'm glad you had a good time this evening at Kezia's. It was very nice of her to have invited you home. I think it did you good".

"You're right, Mom. It did me real good, but now I'm tired. I think I'd better get to bed. Good night".

"Good night, Marissa. Sleep well".

On the way back from taking Marissa home, Kezia's Mom thought it would be nice to meet her parents. Although uncertain as to whether they would accept, they all agreed that inviting the whole family to dinner was worth the try.

Next day, Kezia entered the classroom to find a not-too-pleased Chantelle. She could not get over the idea that her best friend had befriended this totally *not*-happening bore of a girl. When Kezia greeted her, she hesitantly returned her greeting.

"I'm sorry you didn't come to my place yesterday. I know you would have had a great time", Kezia ventured.

"I don't wanna hear about it". Chantelle pouted.

"Okay then, I won't tell you about it, but I think if you get to know Marissa, you'll see that she's actually pretty cool". Kezia smiled, trying to appeal to Chantelle's softer side.

"That's nice", Chantelle replied, not the least bit interested.

As Marissa entered the classroom, Chantelle folded her arms and pressed her lips tightly together, her nose flaring disdainfully.

At break time, Kezia wanted Chantelle to go with her to the cafeteria. She had forgotten to take the snack her Mom had made her, so she decided to have a smoothie instead, but there was no persuading Chantelle. She had no interest in going to the cafeteria with Kezia, if Marissa would be accompanying them. She would also have to sit at the same table with Marissa, and she was not about to do that. She would rather remain in the classroom.

"Would you like anything from the cafeteria?" Kezia asked before leaving.

"No thanks", she responded brusquely.

So Kezia and Marissa went without her. On their way there, she thought of how difficult it must be for Marissa. She searched her mind for a way to help Marissa maintain the positive mood she had gained by spending the past evening with her family.

In addition to her own efforts to be a friend to Marissa, Kezia could think of nothing better than to introduce her to a group of other teenagers that would give her a sense of belonging. She also thought of telling her parents about the abuse, although she knew that by doing so, she would be breaking Marissa's trust.

That was the last thing she wanted to do, but neither did she want to keep a secret that could perpetuate Marissa's pain. Being uncertain as to what she should do, she prayed silently. Then an idea came to her.

"Marissa, what do you normally do on

weekends?"

"What do I normally do?"

"Yeah".

"Nothing special, really. Why?"

"I was just wondering".

"Mostly I read or watch television, listen to some music on my iPod, surf the net, play video games. You know, that kinda stuff".

"I see", Kezia replied pensively.

"I used to go swimming, but I haven't been for a while. Sometimes on Saturdays I go to the mall and window shop".

"Is that fun?"

"Sometimes it is--other times not".

"I hear you. Well, this might seem like even less fun, but would you like to come with me to church on Saturday?"

"Why? What's happening at your church on Saturday?"

"Nothing special. Just regular church service".

"You have regular church service on a Saturday?"

A FUN-FILLED EVENING

"Yes. I go to church every Saturday".

"*Every* Saturday?"

"Yeah!"

"Do you go on Sundays too?"

"No. I only go on a Sunday if there is something special happening, like a wedding, or some other special event".

"I see. I hope you don't mind my saying this, but I find it a bit strange that you go to church every Saturday, but only on special occasions on Sundays".

"No, I don't mind at all, but why do you find that strange?"

"Grandma Beth told me that everyone should go to church on Sunday, because it is the Lord's Day. She says that Sunday is a holy day, because Jesus rose on a Sunday morning. She could not stand to see people going about their regular business on Sundays. She would say that they had no respect for God or for His holy Sabbath day".

"Your grandma Beth seemed to really love the Lord".

"That is true".

"Well, she's right in a sense".

"She is right in a sense? What do you mean?"

"Well, every day is the Lord's day, because He made them all, but the seventh day, which is Saturday, is the only day that He blessed and made holy. The Lord's Day is mentioned once in the Bible, but it was not referring to Sunday".

"My Grandma is *always* right about *everything*. I don't see how she could be so wrong about *that*. I'd really like to know where in the Bible it says that Saturday is a holy day, but we'd better join the line now. We don't want to be late getting back to class". Marissa replied, eying the clock on the wall.

"It's in Exodus. That's the second book of the Bible, and it's in chapter 20, verses 8-11. The word "Saturday" is not in the Bible. It says the seventh day is God's holy Sabbath, and Saturday is the seventh day. We can talk about it later, if you like, but you're right, we'd better hurry up and get our stuff".

"Okay, I'll call you about it later".

A FUN-FILLED EVENING

Having received their purchases with a little time to spare, the two then sat at Marissa's favorite spot in the cafeteria and reminisced for a few minutes, about the events of the previous evening.

"I must tell you again, you have the coolest parents", Marissa reflected, as she sipped her favorite smoothie.

"Thank you". Kezia acknowledged the compliment, but her attention was not all there. Chantelle occupied a large portion of her mind. She could not help feeling somewhat sad. She wanted to help Marissa in whatever way she could, but she also wanted to remain friends with Chantelle. Marissa felt a bit awkward, as she noticed the rift between them. She hoped that they would work things out and resume their friendship. She did not want to get in the way.

Later that evening, Marissa called Kezia, as promised. She was anxious to know where to find the information about God's holy day. She just knew her Grandma was right and that Kezia must have been mistaken. She wanted to clear that up quickly.

"Do you have a Bible?" Kezia asked.

"Yes, Grandma Beth gave me one for my birthday when I was ten, but I've never really opened it to read it. It just looks nice on my dressing table. From time to time, I look at the words she wrote in it to me. That brings back a lot of great memories. So, anyway, where in the Bible did you say that text was found?"

"It's in Exodus, the second book of the Bible—chapter 20, starting at verse 8".

"I am having a hard time believing that she could have missed this information all her life".

"Read it for yourself and tell me what you think".

"I can't wait to check this out on my own".

"Okay then. I'll let you go. Feel free to call me, if you have any questions you think I might be able to answer. If you decide to go to church with me, my Dad will pick you up on Saturday morning. Let me know by Friday".

"Mm, I really don't think so, but I *will* let you know".

"Great! See you tomorrow".

"Okay. See you tomorrow", Marissa replied, thinking, Saturday--a holy day? That is the most ridiculous thing I've ever heard!

As soon as Kezia hung up, she found Exodus 20 and read verses 8-11 as follows:

> Remember the Sabbath day, to keep it holy.
> Six days shalt thou labor, and do all thy work:
> But the seventh day is the sabbath of the LORD thy God: in it thou shalt not do any work, thou, nor thy son, nor thy daughter, thy manservant, nor thy maidservant, nor thy cattle, nor thy stranger that is within thy gates: For in six days the LORD made heaven and earth, the sea, and all that in them is, and rested the seventh day: wherefore the LORD blessed the Sabbath day, and hallowed it.

She could hardly believe her eyes. In astonishment she exclaimed, "The Bible *does* say the seventh day is the Sabbath. Saturday is the seventh day". She wondered if her Grandma Beth

AN ACT OF COMPASSION

knew that there was such a passage in the Bible, and if she had ever read it. There was no question about it, Kezia was right. She was disappointed to discover that her Grandma Beth could really be wrong about something, especially something she had believed all her life. She would have to let Kezia know tomorrow how surprised she was to discover this. Someone distractedly she started on her homework.

FOUR

A New Experience

Later that evening, the telephone rang at the house of the McBrides.

"Hello?" Rebecca answered, panting as she ran from the basement to snatch it before the answering machine came on. She was expecting a call from her co-worker Priscilla, with whom she had been car-pooling, and did not want to miss it.

"Hello, Mrs. McBride. This is Leah Lafontaine".

"Mrs. Lafontaine, hello!" she replied a bit taken aback.

"Leah, please".

"Okay, Leah. Marissa told me she had a great time at your home the other night. Thank you for having her".

"It was our pleasure".

"It was very nice of your daughter to invite her.

It did a lot for her".

"I am happy to hear that. We had a great evening together. We really enjoyed her company".

"From what Marissa has told me, your daughter seems to be a very caring girl".

"Thank you. Kezia loves people".

"That's a wonderful quality in a young person".

"Yes it is. You must be wondering why I called".

"You're right, I'm curious".

"Well, let me not keep you in suspense any longer. After meeting your daughter, we thought it would be nice to meet her parents. I would like to invite your family to dinner some time". By this, Leah hoped that she and Rebecca would become acquainted with each other, while their husbands did the same. She figured that might result in a trusting relationship leading to help for Marissa and her family.

"Oh, thank you". Rebecca replied, pausing for a moment before giving her reply. "That's very kind of you, Leah, but I'm afraid I'll have to pass at this time. It's not a very good time for me. I'm sorry".

A NEW EXPERIENCE

"Rain check then, perhaps?" Leah offered.

"Perhaps. Thank you very much, though. I really appreciate the invitation."

"Our door is always open, if you change your mind. You are welcome any time."

"That's very kind of you. I'll keep it in mind".

Despite Leah's disappointment, she was not surprised that Rebecca did not accept her invitation. She understood the social withdrawal commonly associated with those coping with substance abuse. She had no idea of the physical abuse which further compounded Rebecca's problem, intensifying the tendency to social isolation.

"We just have to keep on praying for them, and keep our door and hearts open to welcome them at their convenience", she later told her husband, as they pondered together how they could help this family.

"Sorry about my parents", Marissa said to Kezia next day at break time. "That was so nice of your Mom to invite our family. My Mom really appreciated it, but she doesn't socialize as she did

AN ACT OF COMPASSION

before. She used to love to entertain and to hang out with her friends, but not anymore".

"Is that because of your Dad?"

"In a way, it is. I mean, he doesn't really tell her she can't go where she wants to, but I don't think she feels comfortable being around people—not like before".

"Do her friends know what's going on with her?"

"They know my Dad lost his job, but I don't think they know the rest of it. Mom does not like to talk about it. I think she wants to avoid all the questions that might come up".

"Well, if she ever changes her mind, and wants to talk to someone, my Mom's a great listener, and she would never repeat anything your Mom told her in confidence. Your Mom would feel very comfortable around my Mom".

"Well, who knows? I don't like to talk about my problems either, but I let you in on what was going on with me—eventually. She might do the same with someone—probably your Mom. I hope she does. I think it would do her a whole lot of good".

"I think so too".

"You know, what you were saying about my going to church with you? I can't believe I'm saying this, but I think I *will* go".

"That's great! I should tell you though, we leave a bit early. Hope that's okay with you".

"How early do you leave?"

"Between 8: 00 and 8:15 am".

"It is kind of early for me, but that should be okay. That passage you gave me about God's holy day? I couldn't believe it. You were right! I was so surprised. I can't wait to hear what Grandma Beth will say when I tell her. I usually write to her in England. She is always happy to receive letters from me by snail mail. She loves to see the envelope with her name on it and to know that it's coming from me, but I think I will call her this time".

Just then, Chantelle showed up. Marissa excused herself, hoping that her absence might give her and Kezia a chance to talk and sort things out.

"Hey, Chantelle. How's it going?" Kezia greeted

her with her usual cheery smile.

"Good", Chantelle replied coolly, taking her seat.

"At least that's something!" Kezia thought. Maybe their next encounter would be an actual conversation, but for now, she would settle for even just a monosyllabic word.

On Saturday morning, the Lafontaines picked up Marissa as arranged. Marissa had not told her parents about her decision to "check out" Kezia's church. She planned to leave home without anyone noticing, but did not know how she would do it, with a car coming to her gate.

That situation worked itself out quite nicely for her. It turned out her Mom had to work, contrary to her original schedule, so she left home early. Her Dad slept in as usual--like a rock. She had no trouble leaving home unnoticed.

As Marissa climbed into the car, she greeted the family with cautious anticipation, looking forward to her new adventure, but uncertain as to what to expect.

"Hi, Marissa!" Kezia greeted her happily. "I'm

glad you decided to come with us".

"Hello Marissa! I didn't think I'd be seeing you again so soon. It's very nice to see you", Kezia's Dad greeted her.

"Hi, Marissa! It's great that you are going to church with us. Hope you will enjoy your visit". Kezia's Mom added.

"Thank you", Marissa smiled, thinking, "What have I got myself into? Ah, relax", she calmed herself, "Kezia is cool, her parents are awesome. If they go to that place every Saturday, it can't be all that bad".

She had no idea how right she was until she got there. The warm welcome she received from everyone, as she entered the building amazed her. Everyone greeted her like a friend. The host at the door handed her a program for the day, and invited her to sign the guest book. Eagerly she accepted. After signing, Kezia led her to the youth class.

Apart from her curiosity, she had no interest in the discussion at first, but as she listened, she found herself becoming interested. She had never been to

AN ACT OF COMPASSION

church, except as a child with her grandmother, and on rare special occasions, like her Uncle Jake's funeral service and her sister, Ashley's wedding. She also attended her nephew's "baptism" when he was a baby. She had also been to Midnight Mass at Christmas a few times, but never a regular church service even on a Sunday, let alone on a Saturday.

Contrary to the awkwardness she thought she would experience, it felt good being in church. She enjoyed the variety and the content of the program, especially the children's story, about David. She thought that was way cool". Her Grandma Beth had told her that story when she was little, but this presentation gave her a better understanding of it, and a greater appreciation for it.

The storyteller recounted how David, a shepherd, defended his people against their oppressors, while only in his mid-teens. He did this by slaying the chief warrior of the enemy's army --a blasphemous, bragging giant named Goliath, who defied the God and the armies of Israel, and taunted the Israelites over a period of forty days.

A NEW EXPERIENCE

So frightful was this man, that even the king could not rise to the challenge when Goliath dared his people, with these boastful words, "I defy the armies of Israel this day; give me a man, that we may fight together".[1] Even the fiercest warriors in the army, including David's elder brothers, shrank in terror at the sight and the words of this monstrous man.

David took up the challenge, and because of his trust in God, conquered Goliath with only a stone and a slingshot, thus winning the victory for his people. The people responded with cheers and chants, ranking David's accomplishment above that of the king.

Hearing the praises of the people toward David, Saul, the king, imagined David to be a threat to his throne, and set out to kill him, hunting him down like an animal. David became a fugitive, taking refuge wherever he could, even escaping into enemy territory, and pretending to be a mad man.

On one occasion, during his pursuit of David, the

---

[1] 1 Samuel 17: 10

AN ACT OF COMPASSION

king became exhausted and went into a cave to rest. There, he fell asleep, not knowing that David and his men were hiding from him in that same cave. David's men saw it as an opportunity to kill Saul and put an end to his relentless efforts to destroy David; but David prevented them from harming Saul.

Instead, he cut off a piece of Saul's garment, and later called out to him to let him know that he had the opportunity to have killed him, but that he had no desire to harm him. "The Lord forbid that I should stretch forth mine hand against the Lord's anointed[1]", David told King Saul, as he held up the piece of garment as proof.

The king wept when he saw how easily David could have killed him, but spared his life. He went away pledging that he would no longer seek David's life.

Not long afterwards, however, the king resumed his pursuit of David, again, falling asleep together with all his men, in very close proximity to David's

---

[1] 1 Samuel 26:11

hiding place. At the king's side was a water bottle and a spear. David took them both, and then called out to the king to let him know that he had spared his life yet again, referring to the king as "my father". He scolded Abner, the king's bodyguard, for sleeping when he should have been protecting his master.

David's bravery, humility, endurance and compassion deeply touched Marissa. "Wouldn't it be wonderful if everyone could be as kind-hearted and courageous as David?" She thought. "I sure would like to be like that".

Later in the program, a melodious song of praise to God, for His great love for humankind, beautifully sung by a husband and wife, also appealed to Marissa. It brought to her a sense of calm and a restfulness that she had never before experienced. It was as if she could feel the love of God surrounding her.

Being in church was becoming more and more a satisfying experience for her. When the pastor took the pulpit, she paid keen attention to the sermon.

AN ACT OF COMPASSION

From that, she learned these very important truths--that human beings are precious in the sight of God; that He excludes no one from being a part of His family; that Jesus Christ offers salvation to all who will accept it.

More importantly, she understood that *she* was special to God. She had previously believed that salvation was only available to certain people, whom God had chosen from birth, or even before that. She had never thought that *she* could ever be one of those people. Now she knew that salvation was a choice, available to everyone through Jesus Christ.

"Kezia", she said after the morning service, "I have to confess. When I came out to the car this morning, I wondered if I had made a mistake deciding to go to church with you guys. Now I'm sure it was no mistake. I'm really glad I came. It's great being here! I thought maybe there would be some strange kind of worship happening, but I liked everything I saw and heard. So far, I think it's *way* cool".

"Good! That's what I was hoping you'd say, but

A NEW EXPERIENCE

there's even more. You'll *love* the evening session! The youth will be conducting it. We will be learning some pretty important stuff".

"Awesome! The only thing is that I can't stay until evening. I want to get home before my parents".

"Aw. How come?" Kezia enquired, disappointed.

"Well, I didn't tell you this, but they don't know that I'm here". Marissa said, somewhat sheepishly.

"Really? How did you manage that?"

"Well, I didn't tell Mom I was coming here because I didn't know how she would react. I was wondering how I would pull it off without her knowing, but it worked itself out. My Mom went to work early this morning, before I woke up. My Dad was asleep when I left, so it was easy to leave without him knowing".

"I see. Okay, come with me. I'll introduce you to my friends now, before you have to leave. You're staying for lunch though, aren't you?"

"Wild horses could not drive me away!"

AN ACT OF COMPASSION

Amid laughter, they headed over to where a group of young people had gathered.

"Hi, Tiffany!" Kezia greeted her spiritedly as Tiffany stood talking to a girl Kezia had never seen before.

"Hey, Kez! What's happening?" Tiffany turned around to give Kezia the broadest smile, as she reached out her long arms and embraced her lovingly. "Kezia, meet my friend, Natalie. She's visiting from California. We met at youth camp last year".

"You met at youth camp? That's awesome! Very nice meeting you, Natalie. Hope you'll like it here. It's great that you kept in touch with each other". Kezia greeted her warmly.

"Nice to meet you too, Kezia. Actually, I like it here very much. My aunt lives here".

"I see. Do you come here often?"

"I usually come once a year".

"That's great! We'll see more of you, then?"

"Hopefully".

"Good. Okay, now it's my turn to introduce.

A NEW EXPERIENCE

Tiffany, Natalie, this is my friend and classmate, Marissa", Kezia announced, placing her arm around Marissa's waist. "She's visiting with us today for the first time".

"That's awesome! Hi, Marissa. Nice to meet you!" Tiffany smiled affectionately, as she extended her hand, clasping Marissa's.

"Nice meeting you, too, Tiffany", Marissa returned.

"Hope you'll come again", Tiffany invited.

"Thank you. I think I will". Marissa smiled.

While Tiffany talked with Kezia and Marissa, Tiffany's brother, Jonathan, came by.

Having overslept, he had missed his ride to church with the family.

"Hi Tiff!" He greeted her cheerfully.

"Well, hey Jonathan! You made it! What time did you get here?"

"I made it in time for the beginning of the sermon".

"That's good. What time did you get up, though?"

"I actually got out of my room just in time to see the back of the car pulling out of the driveway".

"Uh-oh! Didn't you hear when Dad called?"

"Yeah, I heard, and I tried to get up, but I was so tired, I just fell back asleep".

"We didn't want to leave without you, but, you know the rule. After three calls, if you do not budge, you walk. You missed the worship call, the breakfast call and the time-to-go call. Sorry, bro".

"I know, but I was just beat. I had a hard week", Jonathan explained.

"Aw", she responded empathetically "So how did you get here, after all? Did you walk?"

"Not a chance! Thankfully, Craig slept in too. He came and got me".

"Cool. I'm glad you didn't have to walk. I know you had a hectic week. I can see why you would be so tired".

"Thanks, Sis. Thanks for understanding".

"Not a problem. What are sisters for?"

With that he gave her a broad appreciative smile and then turned his attention to Kezia.

"Hey, Kez! How's it goin', girl?" he greeted her affably.

"Hi, Jonathan! It's going great! How about you?" she smiled.

"I'm doin' alright".

"We missed you in the lesson discussion this morning".

"I was late. I missed my ride".

"So I understand. Sorry."

"Thanks. It turned out all right though. I got a little more sleep. By the way, is this your new friend?"

"Oh, I'm sorry. I forgot my manners. Jonathan, this is Marissa. Marissa, Jonathan".

"Nice to meet you, Marissa", Jonathan smiled, reaching out his hand. "I hope you enjoy your visit with us".

"Nice meeting you, too, Jonathan. It's been great so far".

"That's good to know. Do you live around here, or are you visiting from out of town?"

"I live not too far from Kezia. We're

classmates".

"Cool. Hope you'll visit us again".

'Thanks. I think I will", Marissa smiled.

"Okay guys, I'm going over to say hi to Angelica. See you in a bit", Kezia said, as she and Marissa made their way to the next group.

"Yeah, see you later", Jonathan replied, as he headed over to see his friend Will.

As Kezia had a number of friends for Marissa to meet, the introductions continued for a while. After making her rounds with Marissa by her side, she came back to her group, only to hear Jonathan announce, "I'm hungry! Actually, not hungry, starved!"

"What's new?" Tiffany teased. "You're always hungry, always starved".

"Watch it, Sis!" Jonathan returned, faking a threatening look, which generated an outburst of laughter from the group.

"I am with you Jonathan", Kezia agreed. "That aroma from the kitchen is too much for me. Let's go!"

Heading to the lunchroom, the group found their favorite spot vacant, and took their place for lunch.

"This is *delicious*!" Marissa exclaimed, as she savored her second experience with vegetarian cuisine.

"You're right. It's awesome!" Jonathan agreed.

"Is this steak all from plant source, also?" Marissa enquired, incredulously.

"It sure is!" Kezia replied.

"Wow! I'd love to have this at home sometimes". Marissa continued.

"Maybe you can. We have cooking classes for anyone who wants to learn", Kezia offered.

"Really? That's great, but I doubt my Mom would come", Marissa replied.

"It's not only for adults", Kezia explained. "Anyone can participate".

"I'm gonna give that some serious thought", she said, as she took another mouthful.

Marissa felt at home with this friendly group of young people. She could not believe how 'normal' these people were. She liked the way they dressed, looked, interacted with each other, and she *loved* the food! She liked everything she had seen.

She noticed that all the females wore either a skirt or a dress. She had neither, so she had worn a pair of pants. Yet she did not feel out of place. Everyone welcomed her warmly, and no one seemed to even notice her attire. "Are these people awesome, or *what*?" she mused, as she sat there feeling totally at home.

After lunch, Kezia's Dad dropped her home. She missed the company at church, and wished she could have stayed, but knew she would be back before long. Her experience in this new environment was already alleviating the pressures of home. She eagerly looked forward to her next visit.

When Marissa asked to be picked up the following Saturday for church, Kezia gladly consented. During the course of the week, she had told her Mom about her visit there. To her relief, her Mom had no objection, and her Dad would probably not notice, so this time she could spend the whole day without having to sneak back home early. She was happy to be in church again. With no time restriction, she took full advantage of her freedom.

After lunch, she attended the Bible study session, and then the youth program, which she found particularly interesting and informative. It focused on making wise life choices, by following the counsel given in the word of God. This information she considered to be an invaluable tool that would help her in setting goals for her future. That alone made spending the day worthwhile.

Marissa enjoyed the experience so much, that from that day onward, she continued attending church every Saturday with the Lafontaines.

Although she knew that her Mom had no interest in religion, she felt that being in the company of such caring people would be beneficial to her. She wondered if her Mom would ever consider going to church with her at some point. She remembered the pastor's announcement regarding an upcoming evangelistic campaign, and knew that being there would give her a much-needed change of scenery. That would be a great opportunity to invite her, she thought.

When the series began, despite homework, Marissa attended every session. One night, as she returned from hearing a particularly moving sermon, she found her Mom doing laundry in the basement, as she often did on her nights off. That was always a good time to approach her. Folding laundry seemed to have a calming effect on her Mom. Seeing her chance, she summoned up her courage and asked:

"Mom, I'm having such an awesome time at these meetings I've been attending at church. I am learning so many important things. Would you like to come with me?"

"Even if I'd want to, I couldn't. After tonight, I will be on a long stretch of nights. I would not have the time to go there and also get proper rest before I go to work".

"Yes, I know, but you might be able to come for even *one* of the night sessions. They will be going on for a few weeks. If not, you could come with me on Saturday during the day on your weekend off. The meetings are mostly in the evenings, but they continue during the day on Saturdays".

"You're kidding me, right?"

"No, Mom, I'm not kidding. Why would you think that?"

"Do you really think I'd go to church on a Saturday?"

"Why not? It's great going to church on Saturdays!"

"Yeah, right! I think that people who want to go to church should go on Sunday, as the Lord says, not on Saturday! That's how *I* feel about it, but I'm happy that you are going, since you enjoy it so much". Marissa's Mom did not mind her going to church with Kezia. It was a good diversion for her, and she knew Marissa would be in a safe place with the Lafontaines. As for *her*, she could not be *paid* to go to such a place.

"Well, the Lord did not say that people should go to church on Sunday. He said that people should keep the seventh day holy. Saturday is the seventh day", Marissa explained.

"Is that what they tell you?" her Mom retorted.

"Actually, that's what the Bible says", Marissa replied calmly.

"That's plain nonsense", her Mom countered.

"I understand where you're coming from, Mom. When Kezia invited me at first, the idea seemed very strange to me, too. That is why when I decided to go, I didn't tell you, because, even if you would not have objected I didn't want anyone to know I was going there. I was embarrassed, but not anymore".

"What changed your mind?"

"There is something special about being there. I like everything about it".

"Good for you. I know you enjoy the times you spend with Kezia".

"It's not just that. Sure, I went at first just because Kezia invited me and I didn't want to turn her down. Also, I was curious to see what takes place there, and also for something to do while you were at work, except going to the mall or surfing the net… or cleaning the house! Now I go there because I believe it is the place to be".

"I see".

"By the way, did you notice how spotless the house was when you got home that first day that I went to church?"

"That was some time ago. I didn't even know you had been to church".

"I know. I came home before you and Dad, and cleaned everything—not just regular cleaning. I mean *every*thing. I wanted to do something kind, something out of the ordinary--a little bit like David. Now that I know better, though, I think I'll do all that cleaning stuff on Thursdays and Fridays, when I get home from school, instead of on Saturdays, because the Lord says that people should not work on the Sabbath day".

"Well, the way I remember it, Saturday is the day when people clean their houses, do their grocery shopping and things like that, to prepare for Sunday. By the way, I *did* notice that everything was sparkling clean when I got home one Saturday afternoon. I was very pleased. I should have told you. Belated thank you. Who's David, anyway?"

"You know, David the shepherd boy. A young

AN ACT OF COMPASSION

man told that story to the children the first time I went. It was beautiful the way he told it. There was a lesson in it for me".

"That's good. I remember that story". For a brief moment, Rebecca slipped back into her childhood. "Mom told it to me when I was little".

"Grandma told it to me too, when I was little, but when I heard it at church it touched me in a more meaningful way--probably because I am now a teenager, like David was when he showed such bravery and such kindness".

"I see".

The fact that David had made such a significant contribution to his nation at such a young age greatly impressed Marissa and motivated her to aspire to high ideals. His compassion and humility were qualities she also aimed to emulate.

"The people I met at church are really nice and they know the Bible very well", Marissa told her Mom.

"If Saturday is the day that God says people should keep holy, and not Sunday, why do so many

A NEW EXPERIENCE

people go to church on Sunday and hardly anybody on Saturday?" Her Mom wanted to know.

"That's a great question! I had not thought about that".

"Well, maybe you should".

"When Kezia told me what the Bible says about the seventh day, that God blessed and made it holy, I wondered how that could be true. It was hard to accept anything other than what Grandma Beth had told me, but I discovered that God not only blessed the seventh day, He says that we should *remember* to keep it holy.

"He did not say anything about the first day of the week being special. I'm sure there's a reason why most people go to church on Sunday, instead of Saturday, but it's not because God commanded them to keep the first day of the week holy. I don't know the answer to your question yet, but I'm sure I will soon. And by the way, more people go to church on Saturday than you may realize".

"I see. Well, I heard somewhere that we are no longer under the law, but under grace. I heard that

Jesus' death abolished the law. Why should people hold on to something that is outdated?"

"I learned about law and grace in the Bible study group, too, and the way that many people understand it, is different from what the Bible says".

"What do you mean?"

"I learned that God wrote the Ten Commandments with His own finger on tables of stone and gave them to Moses to teach to the people, after He Himself had spoken them in their hearing. In addition to the Ten Commandments, He also gave Moses other laws, which Moses wrote in a book.

"Those laws that Moses wrote in a book are referred to as Moses' Law. They included health laws; laws about sacrifices, which told the people what to sacrifice, when and how to sacrifice; laws regarding how to settle disputes; laws about what is good for food and what is not--things like that. Some of those laws are no longer valid, but the Ten Commandments that God wrote Himself, will never be outdated.

"I see. So which of the laws are outdated then?"

"One law that is definitely done away with is the law of Sacrifices and Oblations".

"The law of *what?*"

"The Law of Sacrifices and Oblations".

"And what is *that*?"

"Oblation means offering, and you know what sacrifice means. I don't yet know all the details, but let me try to explain it as best I can. Before Jesus' crucifixion, the people had to sacrifice animals in order to receive pardon for their sins. So God gave Moses laws that told the people what animals to offer, how to offer them and under what circumstances; but the animals themselves could not take away sin. They were just a symbol of the real Sacrifice--Jesus Christ.

"Jesus came and gave Himself for all the sins of the human race, so that all who confess their sins and ask for forgiveness would receive it. His death took the place of all those animal offerings and sacrifices. Therefore, that law no longer applies. However, the Ten Commandments that God wrote with His own finger can never be changed or abolished. That is why God wrote them on tables of stone, and not in a book, as Moses did with all the other laws. You have heard the saying, 'written in stone', haven't you?"

"Yes, I have".

"What does that mean in your opinion?"

"When something is said to be written in stone, it means it is solid as rock and cannot be altered in any way".

"That's right. That saying probably came from the Bible. God wrote The Ten Commandments in stone with his own finger, and told Moses to put them *inside* a special box called the Ark of the Covenant[1], or the Ark of the Testimony[2], made of wood and overlaid with pure gold. The cover of the box was all of gold, with sculptures of angels carved out of pure gold, stretching their wings across it, and meeting in the middle, as if to guard it.

That box was placed in the inner room of the sanctuary called the Most Holy Place, where only

---

[1] Numbers 10: 33
[2] Exodus 25: 22

A NEW EXPERIENCE

the High Priest could go, and only once a year, to make atonement for the sins of the people. That's how sacred these laws were, and still are, because God does not change. The Ten Commandments will always be valid, because they tell us how to treat our fellow human beings and how to relate to God, our Creator.

"The laws that Moses wrote in a book, the Ceremonial Laws, God told him to put *in the side* of the ark[1], instead of *inside* the ark[2], where the Ten Commandments were placed. Those laws were important too, but they were not as sacred as the Ten Commandments.

Moses' Law was written in a book, instead of on stone because it was temporary. That law was nailed to the cross when Jesus, the true Sacrifice, gave Himself for the redemption of the human race, not the Ten Commandments, as many people believe".

"I see! You really seem to know your stuff, Miss

---

[1] Deuteronomy 31: 26

[2] Exodus 25: 16

AN ACT OF COMPASSION

Bible Student! I hate to admit it, but what you're saying makes a lot of sense. I'm impressed! I did not know that there were two different sets of laws".

"If you want to find out more, you can read it for yourself in the Bible. It's in the book of…"

"That's okay. Thanks anyway". Her Mom quickly interrupted.

"In case you ever want to check it out for yourself, read Deuteronomy 9:10 and Exodus 31:18. Both of these texts say that God wrote the Ten Commandments Himself with his own finger", Marissa said, checking her notes to make sure.

"What's the service like at the church, anyway? I think I would find it strange and boring".

"Come and see. Come with me next time you are free, and tell me what you think".

"Ah, I don't think so. I'm really not religious. You can keep going, but I think I'll pass".

"Okay, but if you change your mind…"

"I doubt it".

"Okay, but you don't know what you're missing".

"Oh, well, I'll take my chance".

A week later, Marissa had a conversation on the phone with Kezia regarding a Bible prophecy seminar she had seen advertised.

"Hi Kezia", the conversation went, "I saw a sign on the church's billboard about a Bible prophecy series scheduled for the middle of October. What's that all about?"

"Bible prophecies are revelations that God gave to His servants, telling them of certain events that will happen at different times in earth's history. The series deals with prophecies about things that will happen as we approach the end of time", Kezia replied.

"The end of time?" Marissa asked with a puzzled expression. She had never heard of that concept before, and never thought there could be such a thing as time coming to an end. She had heard that Jesus would return to earth some day, but did not understand it to mean that time would end at His return.

"Yes, Jesus tells us in His word that the world in

AN ACT OF COMPASSION

which we now live will end when He returns to receive His faithful followers. He tells us that certain things will happen to let us know when that time is near. Even before Jesus came to earth the first time, prophets of old had predicted some of the things that would happen in the last days of earth's history. Many of these things have already happened, but there is more to come".

"What kinds of things?"

"I can't explain it all, but the Bible says that certain signs will tell us when the end is near, and many of those signs have been, or are now being fulfilled".

"That sounds frightening!" Marissa replied, finding it hard to process the idea that this world could really end some day. She had learned in school about things that this generation could do to preserve the environment for the coming generations. To think that the Bible foretold the end of the world was inconceivable to her.

"You don't need to be afraid", Kezia reassured her. "Jesus says that when His followers see these things happening they should look toward heaven, because it means that His coming is near, when all the bad things will end, and He will take us to heaven to live with Him forever. As for the signs, they are things like increase in violence and crime, disturbances in nature such as terrible floods, earthquakes and tsunamis in different places. Those are some of the signs".

"Where in the Bible does Jesus speak about the signs of the end?"

"You can read about them in Matthew 24".

"Matthew 24?"

"Yes, at least that's one of the places".

"Thank you. I really would like to know more about the signs that tell us that this world will come to an end. I'm finding it a little hard to believe. I'll look it up as soon as I get a chance. Matthew 24, right?"

"Yes, that's right".

"So Matthew 24 is just one of the places in the Bible that talks about the end of time? There are other scriptures on the subject?"

"Yes. There are other books of the Bible that talk about that—like the book of Daniel and the book of Revelation, but Matthew is a good place to start".

"That's great. Thank you".

As soon as Marissa got off the phone, she rushed to her room for her Bible. She could not wait to read about the end of time. It sounded a bit like science fiction to her. Little did she know that her Mom had beaten her to it.

Having heard Marissa's questions to Kezia about the signs of the end, her curiosity got the better of her. She started reading Matthew 24 on the internet, while Marissa was still on the phone. She had satisfied her curiosity, but what she read did not make much of an impression upon her.

"What's new about earthquakes and violence in the earth?" she thought. "Those things have been happening for centuries". Yet the thought of knowing what else the Bible had to say about the future intrigued her. She had noticed the doomsday headlines of magazines on the newsstands and never paid much attention to their claims. She knew that was just hype.

"What will *this* speaker have to say?" She really wanted to know. She thought he might be another one of those hell-fire preachers who try to scare the congregation to death, or to life, as he might put it. He was not going to scare *her*, though. She was prepared. Unable to contain her curiosity, she planned, unknown to Marissa, that she would make every effort to attend these sessions whenever she could, if at all possible.

She was not planning to attend the evangelistic series, but she sure wanted to attend those end time prophecy seminars. She knew that things could not continue the way they were going, and wondered what the solution was. Something had to change, but, the end of the world? The return of Jesus Christ? She didn't think so!

FIVE

A Step Forward

To Marissa's total surprise and delight, her Mom told her of her decision to accompany her to the prophecy series whenever she could. Although she had not disclosed it to Marissa previously, she had secretly entertained the idea of going just once, only to please her, and to satisfy her own curiosity. She did not know for sure, if she would actually do it, or when, but she had thought about it. Now she *really* wanted to.

Her schedule would not allow her to go to any of the night meetings during the seminars, so she would have to go during regular church hours. Now she would not hesitate. She wanted so much to hear what this preacher had to say about the future of this world, that she would go back on her word about never going to church on a Saturday, if necessary.

There was one problem, though. How would she pull it off without her husband knowing?

She had to devise a plan. She would dress in her usual Saturday morning attire, go to the church, load up the car with groceries on her way back home, and he would be none the wiser, she figured. He would just think she had gone shopping, as she usually did whenever she had Saturdays off.

If he should awaken before she left, she could just pretend she was taking Marissa to church on her way shopping. Besides, he knew that she occasionally met her friend Priscilla for brunch or for mid-morning coffee. She could also cover her tracks that way.

But what if he would actually ask where she was going? She would not want to lie. As it turned out, she did not need to give an explanation. On the morning she decided to go, the solution came naturally. Her husband was in a sleep state out of which, not even the loudest peal of thunder could have jolted him. She and Marissa went through the door without a hitch.

So, with reserve and without her husband's knowledge, Rebecca accompanied her daughter to church. If she became bored, she reasoned, or if she thought the happenings were too strange for her liking, she would just slip out quietly and leave. She knew Marissa would get a ride home, the same way she did at other times, so she did not have to worry about that. She prepared herself for a quick escape.

What she found, however, was nothing like she had imagined. Her first surprise was the welcome she received. Everyone greeted her with such warmth it was as if she had been a long lost friend or relative.

Because of the verbal and physical abuse from her husband, she had been feeling insecure around people. With this group, she felt completely at ease. Everyone made her feel as if she belonged, as if she really mattered. "What a wonderful feeling!" she thought.

It was nothing like the bunch of stiff, rigid people, looking dour and severe, centuries behind in fashion and unwelcoming to outsiders that she had pictured. "How wrong I was!" she thought, as she basked in the flood of positive attention she was receiving.

Although all who greeted her were impeccably dressed in beautiful and even fashionable clothes-- the men in suits and ties and the women in lovely dresses or skirt suits, no one seemed to notice her jeans and T-shirt. They just showered her with warm embraces and handshakes. "What a great way to start a day!" she thought, eager to see what was yet to come.

After the initial greeting, one of the women invited her to sign the guest book. As she stood with pen in hand about to sign, the pastor, passing by, noticed her.

"Hello, Madam. I am Pastor Pottinger. Welcome! It's great to have you with us today". His radiant smile and his warm, firm handshake, gave her an added feeling of security.

"It's a pleasure meeting you, Pastor Pottinger. I'm Rebecca Mc Bride". Immediately she felt a connection with the pastor. He seemed so genuine.

"Good to meet you, Rebecca. I hope you will have a wonderful day with us".

"I believe I will. Thank you!"

"I am always curious as to what brings our first time visitors to us. I hope you don't mind my asking how you came to know about us".

"No. I don't mind at all! My daughter has been attending for some time. I came with her today".

"I see. What's your daughter's name?"

"You probably wouldn't know her. Her name is Marissa".

"Oh, yes! Marissa! Of course! She comes with Kezia! It's wonderful having her here. By the way, I know everyone who comes through these doors. I make it my business to know, and I reserve a special greeting for our visiting friends", he smiled.

It greatly impressed Rebecca that the pastor took the time and the interest to become acquainted with everyone who came to the church. His concern for the well-being of others was evident. If she should become interested in associating with any church, this one would be high on her list.

A STEP FORWARD

She had only conversed briefly with the pastor, but she was starting to feel she could confide in him. She had a great first impression of all that she had encountered so far, but his kind, gentle manner had made her feel even more at ease.

While she talked with him, she noticed that there was a steady stream of people coming in. As she finished her conversation and started to make her way in, an usher greeted her and escorted her to her desired seat. She requested to sit where she could reserve a seat for Marissa, who joined her at the end of the youth class. By this time, she felt so comfortable she was in no hurry to leave. She remained for the sermon, and what she learned astounded her.

She had no idea of the events predicted in the prophetic books of Daniel and the Revelation, and the accuracy of their fulfillment in world history. That motivated her to do her own research. She also learned that the natural disasters of the last days, foretold in Matthew 24, were not just everyday occurrences, as it had appeared when she first read the chapter.

She now understood that as it came nearer to the end of time, they would be occurring with greater frequency and intensity than at any other time in history. She was greatly surprised to learn that the 2011 tsunami in Japan was so powerful that it shortened the days by 6.8 microseconds, and shifted the earth's axis by seven centimeters, and that other massive earthquakes have had a similar effect[1]. She pondered these things, but something more immediate occupied her thoughts.

After leaving the church, the idea kept coming to her that the pastor might be able to help her family in some way. The following day, she called and made an appointment to meet with him at a convenient time. He arranged to meet with her on Wednesday at 9.00 a.m. in his office, the only vacant time slot on his crowded calendar for the week.

That was the ideal time for her. She could go there right after her night shift. After leaving the

---

[1] Alan Buis (NASA)
Jet Population Laboratory, Pasadena, CA

pastor's office, she would stop at the grocery store and pick up a few items. Then, on her way home, she would collect some clothes she had dropped off at the dry cleaner's. That would eliminate any questions as to her whereabouts. She eagerly awaited the day.

After a long and tiresome Tuesday night working the graveyard shift, Wednesday morning finally came. Rebecca headed for the locker room and quickly changed into her street clothes. On her way out the door, she waved to Priscilla, who was just on her way to the locker room.

They were not going to be having coffee together in the cafeteria this morning before heading home, as usual, but she did not give an explanation, only that she had to leave.

With some apprehension, she arrived at the church as arranged. She got there a little early and sat in the car sorting out her thoughts. At exactly 9:00 am, she knocked on the office door. Expectantly the pastor answered the knock. With an enthusiastic handshake and his characteristic warm smile, he greeted her. Motioning to the chair in front of his desk, he invited her to take a seat.

After inquiring about her well-being and that of her family, and conversing briefly with her about the weather and traffic on the way, he invited her to join him in seeking the Lord's guidance in their discussion. He was as curious about this meeting as Rebecca was nervous. Prayer and small talk now over, he was ready to listen.

"Now, Mrs. McBride", he asked gently, his kind eyes meeting hers, as he placed his hands on the table, leaning forward, "How may I be of service to you today?"

Somewhat haltingly, Rebecca began, giving him a general description of her situation at home. Although it was difficult for her to divulge such matters, she felt she had to do it. It was no use continuing to keep it a secret; and who better to talk to than a pastor? She told him about the alcoholism, the abuse and their financial dilemma. She explained also, that she was interested in counseling, but that her husband would not hear of it. She did not know what to do. Divorce seemed the only solution, she told him, but that was not her desire.

The pastor offered words of encouragement and expressed his belief in the power of prayer to turn around even the most seemingly impossible situation. He offered to visit and pray with the family. She would like that, she told him, but she greatly doubted that her husband would consent. The pastor understood. He prayed inwardly that the Lord would intervene and give him the wisdom he needed in order to help this family.

After leaving the meeting, Rebecca pondered how she could arrange for the pastor to visit. She did not know how, but felt sure that there had to be a way.

"Thank you for taking the time to meet with me, Pastor", she said, as she reached out her hand in a parting handshake. "It has been a great help".

"It was my pleasure. I will be praying for you and your family", he responded reassuringly.

She left the pastor's office feeling so comforted, she did not want to miss the opportunity of having

AN ACT OF COMPASSION

him visit and pray for the family. On her way home, her all-consuming thought was how she would tell her husband that she had met with the pastor, and that he had offered to visit their home.

She had not yet even told him that she had been to the church. Had he known, he might have objected, and the last thing she wanted was to make him angry. She was not used to praying, and did not know how, but now she definitely needed some divine help. What should she do? She had no reason to think that God would answer a prayer coming from someone like her, even if she knew how to pray.

In utter desperation, she exclaimed: "O God, help me! I don't know what to do". Almost immediately, the idea came to her that she should invite the pastor and tell her husband afterwards. "Could that be God's answer?" she wondered. "My husband would be *furious* if I did that!"

Just then, she remembered how anxious he became whenever he had an appointment he would rather not keep. She recalled his last dental visit. In order not to have lost sleep over it, he had chosen a convenient day, and then called the dentist's office to see if there were any cancellations for that day, so he could get in at the last minute. Based on experience, she was certain that even if he would consent to meet with the pastor, it would be a constant worry for him, right up to the appointed time.

"That's the answer!" she exclaimed excitedly. "Thank You God!"

She did not think of her utterance as a prayer, just an expression of despair, but she was sure that God had heard and answered. She would invite the pastor one evening when she was on the day shift, and when her husband would likely be at home. As soon as she stepped in the door, she called the pastor and made the appointment.

With great trepidation, she awaited the day. She would have preferred to have been able to use the direct approach with her husband, but she would do whatever she had to. *Something* had to change.

The day came for the pastor's visit, and Rebecca

had still not told her husband. He knew that something was up, because her anxiety was evident throughout the evening. She had hurried home from work, prepared dinner a little earlier than usual, vacuumed the living room floor, which did not appear necessary.

After she and Marissa had made the kitchen sparkling clean, she put a fresh bouquet of flowers from the garden on the centre table, showered, changed her clothes and fixed her hair. It was not Marissa's birthday, was it? He hoped not. Was it hers?

He knew his drinking sometimes affected his memory, but he hoped it hadn't gone that far. As the time drew closer, Rebecca grew more anxious. She could not delay any longer; she had to tell him now; but how? "Just say it!" She told herself. Then, summoning up all of her courage, she did. His reaction did not surprise her.

"You did what!" he growled. "You invited a *pastor* here? Are you kidding me! I don't want any preacher coming into *my* house. He's not coming here to tell me how to run my business. You'd better call him back and cancel!"

Rebecca decided to risk his fury. She stood firm. The outcome of this evening might well decide their future as a family. She very much wanted the family to remain together, but not like this.

"He'll be here in half an hour", she said calmly, maintaining her resolve. "I think it will be good for us".

"In half an hour! Are you out of your mind?" he ranted.

"Sometimes it's better not to have too much time in advance to do certain things. It's less worry", she said, trying hard to be tactful, so as not to trigger an episode right before the pastor's arrival. "The pastor is not coming here to interfere", she continued, attempting to put his mind at ease. "He's a very nice person. He really cares about people".

"You think he's nice, huh? Well, *you* seem to like him. *You* can talk to him. I am keeping out of his way, and he'd better keep out of mine!" he warned, as he reached for his cigarettes and lighter.

AN ACT OF COMPASSION

Making his way to the kitchen, he grabbed a bottle of beer, slammed the refrigerator door furiously and stormed out, retreating to the adjoining room. Slamming that door shut, he slumped down into the couch, opened his beer and took a huge gulp, swishing it around in his mouth before swallowing, as if trying to wash away the very idea of a pastor being in his house.

"Of all the people in the world--a *pastor*! She invited a *pastor* here. What an audacity!" He fumed. "Good for him I have this little hideaway". This little hideaway was their elder daughter's room before she married and moved away. He could not figure what got into his wife to make her invite a preacher to their home. Yet he could not bring himself to throw him out. He would just hang out in his pad, relax, and calm his mind.

Pastor Pottinger arrived on the dot of 6:45 p.m., as arranged. Rebecca met him in the driveway.

"Hello, Pastor", she greeted him, trying to be cheerful. "Thank you for coming".

"My pleasure", he smiled, as he reached out and

shook her hand. "How are you?" he asked with interest.

"I'm fine, thank you, and you?" she responded politely.

"To God be the glory. I am very well, thank you", he replied, unconvinced by her claim to be "fine".

Sensing that something was not right, he asked again, "How *are* you, really?"

"I'm sorry; my husband will not be joining us this evening", she replied, evading the question, but unable to conceal her uneasiness. "I hope I haven't wasted your time", she added apologetically.

"Not at all! You have not wasted my time. It's good to see you. Hello, Marissa! Good to see you! How are you?" he called, as Marissa came toward them.

"Hi Pastor! I'm good, thank you. It's good to see you, too!"

"Actually, Mrs. Mc Bride, I hope to meet your husband at some future time, but for now, I would not mind spending a little time chatting with you and

Marissa. Is that okay?"

"That's quite okay. I was greatly encouraged by your words during our meeting. I would not mind a few more words of encouragement at this time".

"Good! There are lots more where those came from", he smiled, as they walked together up the steps to the door of the house.

"Come on in!" she invited, as she opened the shiny wooden door of the comfortable brown brick house, which occupied an unusually large corner lot. With every nerve in her body she tried to maintain her calm, knowing how angry her husband was, and that he was still in the house.

"Thank you", he smiled, as he stepped inside.

"Have a seat, please". She motioned to the ivory-colored leather chair that sat by the wall, facing a beautiful painting of a garden in bloom.

"Thank you, but before I sit, I would like to pronounce a blessing upon your household in the name of the Lord Jesus Christ".

"Please do! Thank you!" Rebecca readily accepted.

The Pastor prayed, inviting the presence of the Lord and His holy angels to the dwelling of the McBride family. He asked for protection, blessings and peace upon their household, and for the Lord's guidance during the course of his visit. That prayer seemed to have ushered in an air of calm and tranquility. Before sitting, the pastor looked briefly around the room, his eyes settling on the picture opposite his chair.

"What a lovely painting!" he exclaimed. "That garden looks so real, it makes me want to walk right in and pick some flowers". That generated a burst of laughter.

"Thank you. That's true; it *is* very life-like. In the winter, when I look at it, it reminds me of spring and always lifts my spirits, no matter how gloomy the weather", Rebecca replied.

"I can imagine. I see that you have quite the taste for good art".

"Thank you. I do appreciate art that captures beautiful scenes of nature".

"Do you do any painting yourself?"

"No-o", she chuckled. "The last time I painted anything was in Kindergarten. I'm sure I got more of the paint on my clothes than on the paper".

"I see. Would it be accurate to say that you are much better at planting than at painting, then?"

"That would be accurate", she smiled.

"Your garden is beautiful. I couldn't help noticing it as I drove up", he commented, looking through the window at the carefully sculpted and meticulously color-coordinated garden that occupied a large portion of the oversized lot. "You must put a lot of work into it. Have you lived here long?"

"Thank you. I do put a lot of work into my garden, and yes, we've lived here for a number of years. Marissa was born in this house".

"I see. Now, tell me, Marissa, do you remember that event?" The laughter that resulted from that question provided the perfect segue into the discussion that followed.

"It's good to be able to share a moment of laughter", the pastor said. "You see, 'a merry heart doeth good like a medicine: but a broken spirit drieth the bones' ".

"Pastor, I'm curious. Where did that saying come from? Did you just make it up?" Marissa asked, as the laughter subsided.

"No, I did not make it up. It came straight from the Bible!"

"Really? Can you tell us where to find it?"

"I certainly can! You will find it in the book of Proverbs. It's in chapter 17 and verse 22".

"Thank you. The Bible is awesome. It says the neatest things", Marissa smiled.

"You're right. The word of God *is* awesome. It has instructions for every area of our lives".

"Every area?" Marissa asked, wondering if the Bible could instruct her on how to get an "A" on the French test she would be taking first thing in the morning.

"That's right--every area", the pastor affirmed.

"Really? Does it have instructions to help students succeed?" Marissa asked, wide-eyed.

"Yes, it does. Do you have anything specific in mind?" he asked.

AN ACT OF COMPASSION

"Well, I have a difficult French test tomorrow, and I really want to get an "A" on it. Is there something in the Bible that could help me?"

"Philippians 4: 13 is one text that comes to mind right away. Let's find it and see what it says?"

"Philippians?"

"It's in the New Testament after the book of Ephesians; that's a few books after the gospel of John. Here, I'll help you with that". Reaching for her Bible, the pastor found the verse and returned it to her. While he turned the pages, Marissa watched closely, observing the books as he flipped passed them. As she read it, she became very excited.

"'I can do all things through Christ which strengtheneth me'. That's awesome! Thank you!"

"You're welcome. The God who created us is interested in every aspect of our well-being, even the simple things. He didn't just create us and leave us alone to fend for ourselves", the pastor satd.

"Is God really that interested in people?" Rebecca asked, a bit surprised that God would give consideration to a child's desire to do well on a test.

"He certainly is. He is never too busy for us. He cares about everything that concerns us".

"If I wanted to read something that tells me that God cares about my well-being, where in the Bible would I look?" Rebecca asked.

"A good place to start would be Matthew Chapter 6 starting at verse 25. Let's find it and see what it says".

"I've got it!" Marissa said, after just a few seconds.

"That was real quick, Marissa!" the pastor commended her. "*We* are still turning".

"I'm there now", Rebecca said as she settled on the page.

"Okay. Rebecca would you read for us, please?"

Reading from the King James Version, she began:

> "'Therefore I say unto you, Take no thought for your life, what ye shall eat, or what ye shall drink; nor yet for your body, what ye shall put on. Is not the life more than meat, and the body than raiment? Behold the fowls of the air: for they sow not, neither do they reap, nor gather into barns; yet your

heavenly Father feedeth them. Are ye not much better than they? Which of you by taking thought can add one cubit unto his stature? And why take ye thought for raiment? Consider the lilies of the field, how they grow; they toil not, neither do they spin: And yet I say unto you, that even Solomon in all his glory was not arrayed like one of these. Wherefore, if God so clothe the grass of the field, which today is, and tomorrow is cast into the oven, shall he not much more clothe you, O ye of little faith? Therefore take no thought, saying, what shall we eat? Or what shall we drink? Or, wherewithal shall we be clothed?'"

"Okay. Let's skip to verse 33", the pastor interjected.

"But seek ye first the kingdom of God, and his righteousness; and all these things shall be added unto you'".

"Well read. So, you see, God loves and provides for all His creatures, even the tiniest of them. How much more those He created in His own image and for whom He died! He takes care of all who put their trust in Him. In fact, He takes care even of those who do not know Him or serve Him. Matthew 5: 45

tells us that 'He causes His sun to rise on the evil and the good, and sends rain on the righteous and the unrighteous'" (NASB).

"It sounds as if God really cares a lot about people", Rebecca concluded.

From his hiding place in the guest room, Matthew could hear the gentle words the pastor spoke, as he talked with his wife and daughter. He could sense the genuine interest he had in their well-being. Rebecca asked more questions about the Bible, about heaven, about salvation and about God.

The more the pastor spoke about God, the less her reservations about Him became. She was beginning to think of Him as a loving caring being, rather than a vindictive despot looking over the earth, with the intent of catching and punishing those who did not follow His rules.

She had always wondered how people became "saved". Not that she thought salvation would apply to her; she had just wondered about it, so she asked the pastor.

In answer to her questions, he directed her to

AN ACT OF COMPASSION

several Bible passages, which she and Marissa took turns reading. Matthew heard his wife read the words of Jesus in John 6: 37, and the pastor's explanation that salvation in God's kingdom was equally available to everyone. Jesus died for all, he assured her. Therefore, He will never turn away any one who repents and turns to Him.

"There are many other texts in the Bible which tell us that salvation is a free gift, available to *all* who will accept it, but one of the most profound statements of Jesus regarding salvation is found in the book of John", The pastor continued. "Let's turn there. That's the last book of the gospels. So, there's Matthew, then Mark, then…"

"Oh, I know where to find it!" Marissa interrupted eagerly.

"Very good, Marissa! I can see that you are an A student in the Bible class you have been attending.

"I've been learning a lot", Marissa agreed, her smile broadening.

"That's great! Keep up the good work", the Pastor encouraged. "There's no better way for a young person to spend her time. In fact, there is no better way for *anyone* to spend his time than in the study of the word of God. Let us go to chapter three then, and we will read verse 16. Marissa, would you read that verse for us, please?"

"Certainly!" she replied, as she read, 'For God so loved the world that He gave His only begotten Son, that whosoever believeth in Him should not perish, but have everlasting life'".

Listening intently through the wall, as Marissa read, Matthew thought, "Oh, really? Whoever believes in God will have everlasting life? That's because He has never met *me*!"

"So anyone who believes in Jesus can be saved?" Rebecca asked.

"That's right! Everyone has the opportunity to choose. God wants everyone to live with Him in heaven, but it is up to each person to decide. All who accept Jesus as their Savior, and do as He teaches, will be saved and live with Him forever", the pastor replied.

"So you mean *I* have just as good a chance to be

saved as *you* do?" Rebecca asked incredulously.

"That's right! One human being is just as precious in the sight of God as another. He loves us all equally", the pastor informed her.

"That's awesome!" Rebecca replied.

"It is indeed", he agreed.

"I'm sure that could not apply to me. God has no use for *my* kind", Matthew thought, as he listened with an equal blend of anger and grief. "I'm just too messed up". Fastening his ear to the wall, he listened, as the discussion continued. After a few more minutes, the pastor announced:

"It is always difficult to bring a Bible discussion to a close, but hopefully, we will do this again soon. It has been a pleasure spending this time with you both", he said, as he prepared to leave.

Before leaving, he read Psalm 91, which speaks of God's protection and deliverance for those who put their trust in Him. Matthew, his ear still fastened to the wall, listened with increased interest.

The words of the psalm made a deep impression upon him. He wondered if God would deliver *him*.

He desperately needed deliverance. The pastor had read that God would deliver those who put their trust in Him and call upon Him. That would rule him out, he thought. How could he trust in God when he doubted that He even existed? Yet the idea of a God who could deliver him from his circumstances greatly appealed to him.

He hated his life. He hated being a slave to that bottle. He hated himself because of it. He hated himself for hitting his wife and his daughter. He hated the fact that he could not adequately provide for his family. He wanted desperately to change, but knew he could not help himself, and hated himself even more for being so helpless. He hated, he hated, he hated! "Something's gotta give", he told himself. "Could this be the answer for me?" he wondered. "Would God help *me*?"

"With long life will I satisfy him, and show him my salvation", he heard the pastor say, as he concluded his reading of the psalm.

"I would like to find that salvation", Matthew mused. "I would like to be saved, even if only from myself. At the rate I'm going, I'm about to self-destruct. Who would not want to be satisfied with a long, happy life? If I continue to drink this way, I certainly cannot look forward to that!"

"Mrs. McBride, Marissa, I hope you will hold on to the promises of God in this psalm, and the other verses we looked at tonight", the pastor said, as he closed his Bible.

"Those words gave me a lot to think about", Rebecca nodded reflectively.

"I had already memorized John 3: 16. I like that text a lot. It gives me a very warm feeling inside, to think that God loves me so much, that He made such a great sacrifice to save me", Marissa added.

"Yes, that is absolutely wonderful. God's love for us is truly amazing. Well, I hope we will be able to meet again soon, perhaps with all of the family. As we began, so we shall end. Let us pray". The pastor prayed for everyone in the family individually, putting them by name before the Lord. Matthew turned off his thoughts and directed his full attention to the prayer, as he heard the Pastor say:

A STEP FORWARD

"...and Father God, let Your mercies be upon your precious child Matthew. Deliver him from the prison of that bottle".

His heart melted as he heard the words. Normally, he would have been very angry, in fact, livid that his wife had told the pastor about his drinking problem. That did not matter now. In fact, he felt relieved that she had told him. Someone else now shared his burden.

He felt no condemnation in the tender words of the pastor, only a profound sense of compassion. The mention of his name in prayer touched him in a way he had never experienced before. It deeply consoled him. It released in him emotions he never knew he had

The pastor, on the other hand, having no awareness of Matthew's presence in the house, wanted to leave before he returned home. The idea of being the recipient of Matthew's charged fist did not particularly appeal to him. Rebecca had thought it strange that he had not stormed off to the bar in his usual manner, instead of the guest room. Matthew,

AN ACT OF COMPASSION

in the meantime, still listening intently, closed his eyes tightly, trying to fight back the tears, as the pastor concluded his prayer with a special plea for him.

"Merciful, Almighty God, release Matthew from the shackles that enslave him, and give him the victory over that oppressive addiction, that seeks to rob him of the fulfillment of Your intended purpose for his life. Help him to come to the realization of Your great love for him, and of Your desire for his good. I know that there is no problem too hard for You to solve. In the multitude of Your tender mercies and by Your great power, bind up the wounds, and restore this family to unity, to health and to prosperity.

"Let now Your protection and Your peace rest upon this household. Thank You for granting this petition, for I ask it in the saving, healing name of Jesus Christ, Your only begotten Son, to Whom be glory forever, Amen".

As the pastor ended his prayer, Matthew's tears began to flow, but with them, his hope began to grow. Someone understood his desperation. Someone cared. That gave him a tremendous sense of peace.

Instead of anger toward his wife, Rebecca, he felt a deep sense of gratitude. He could not figure out why he had not gone to the bar tonight; he had every reason to have left the house, but now he was glad that he had stayed.

After the pastor left, he remained in his hiding place for a while, drying his tears and regaining his composure. He tried to figure out a way to pretend he was still angry at Rebecca, so she would not know that he had been listening, and had been affected by what he had heard, but that was impossible.

Reflecting on the words of the pastor, he experienced a calm that eroded from his mind every negative emotion. "Having a pastor here was not such a bad idea, after all", he thought, as he left the room and silently closed the door behind him.

SIX

PERSISTENT KNOCK

Following the pastor's visit, peace seemed to have settled over the McBride household. Rebecca kept going over in her mind the words from the Bible that Pastor Pottinger had shared with her and her daughter, particularly focusing on the knowledge that Jesus accepts anyone who comes to Him. As she pondered the idea, she began to experience a great sense of excitement at the thought that that included her.

"I'd better make a note of where that text is found", she thought, as she prepared breakfast the morning after the visit. She had made a note in her diary of the texts that they had read, but she wanted to have certain ones always in plain view.

Reaching up to the calendar on the wall, she wrote in her own words under the current date,

"John 3:16: Anyone who believes in Jesus will have everlasting life". Under the next day's date, she wrote, "John 6: 37: Jesus will never turn away anyone who comes to Him". Although she had not yet committed these texts to memory word for word, she had the main idea, and wanted to etch them indelibly into her mind.

That was not the way she had always understood it. Her previous belief was that the fate of all human beings was determined the moment they came into the world, or even before; that no one knew for sure what his or her lot would be until the Judgment Day, that is, if God really existed, which she had seriously doubted. She had previously believed that only on that day she would know whether she would go to heaven or hell, and she had greatly doubted that God would ever have chosen her for heaven, if in fact, he did exist. She was sure she would not have been that lucky.

She now knew that going to heaven did not depend on luck; that it was all up to her. She now knew that salvation was not like the lottery, or some

AN ACT OF COMPASSION

other game of chance--that all who chose to accept that precious gift had the guarantee that they would receive it. She now understood that Jesus had already paid the price for *her* salvation. She needed only to claim it. "What an amazing discovery! What a wonderful enlightenment!" she reflected. She wanted to know more.

Following the pastor's visit, Rebecca made another discovery. She noticed that something was definitely different about her husband. Maybe the change was not in him, she thought. Maybe *her* perspective had changed. Maybe she was just seeing him through different eyes, she told herself.

Nevertheless, she could not deny the fact that he seemed calmer, more patient, not as easily irritated and more positive. Was he actually being more considerate and courteous to her and to their daughter? Or was she suffering from an over-active imagination? Was it just in her mind that there was less tension between them, and that he seemed more relaxed and more at peace with himself? Or was it really true? The passing of time confirmed the

THE PERSISTENT KNOCK

accuracy of her observation.

Unquestionably, something significant had happened to Matthew. Something *was* different about him, and whatever it was, she liked it. His reliance on alcohol seemed to have decreased. He even seemed to be smoking less. Now she could even have a conversation with him without being anxious that he might become angry at the slightest provocation. She wondered what had brought about the change, but thought it best not to rock the boat by asking.

Rebecca treasured the words from the Bible that she had learned from the pastor. They were not just comforting for the moment. They remained with her constantly. As the days went by, she developed a growing interest in studying the word of God for herself. She could hardly believe it. If someone had told her a few short weeks ago that she would be reading the Bible, she would have thought that the poor thing had flown the coop. She would have been certain that she had found the one who flew over the cuckoo's nest. Now, she was even interested in

AN ACT OF COMPASSION

joining the Bible study group with her daughter. She also looked forward to future visits with this welcoming group of people, and to hearing the word of God being spoken and sung. She knew she could not be in church very often, because of her work, but whenever she could, she wanted to attend.

On her next weekend off, she awoke early Saturday morning, and started getting ready for church. She needed no invitation this time. In fact, she was ready before her daughter, and sat waiting for her to finish getting dressed. She wanted to be on time for the first session, where the congregation divided into groups to discuss the Bible lessons they had studied during the week. This discussion was often so captivating that the teacher sometimes had difficulty bringing it to a close. She wanted to be a part of that. She wanted to learn everything she could about the Bible.

As she sat waiting in the living room, she heard the heavy footsteps of her husband making his way down the stairs. She wondered what he might say, or what he might do, if he knew that she was going to church, especially on a Saturday. He had become aware that Marissa was going there and did not mind. He considered it a safe way for her to spend a part of her weekend, since she would be with other young people, who were not likely to get her into any kind of trouble. He was not the ideal father, and he knew it, but he cared deeply about his daughter's wellbeing. He had welcomed the weekly visits to church as a good diversion for Marissa, an alternative to the mall; but for *her*, it might be a different matter.

She did not want any trouble, so she would rather he did not know. She had hoped she would be able to slip out and leave before he awoke, but, oops! Here he comes! On her previous visit, she had taken the precaution to have dressed very casually, so he would have had no reason to suspect that she was going anywhere outside of the usual, but today was different. He would definitely know she was up to something special. Should she hide the book she was reading, as she sat waiting, and waiting, and waiting, for what now seemed like an eternity for

AN ACT OF COMPASSION

her daughter to complete her endless primping?

He knew she had wanted to visit the church to satisfy Marissa. He probably figured out by now that she had actually done it. How else would the pastor have visited their home at *her* invitation? How would he take it, though, if he knew that she was actually serious about going to church, and maybe even becoming a part of it? How would he react if he knew that she was reading the Bible, and that she wanted to know more about God? He had never believed that there was a God, she recalled. He would always say that God was a figment of the imagination of softies, looking for a crutch, a way to escape the harsh realities of life. There could be no relationship, or experience with God, as people claim; you can only experience that which you can prove to exist, he would argue, to which she would agree. How would he react to her new frame of mind? Would he think she was stupid? He would certainly be surprised! Would he be angry? Should she prepare for another episode? All these thoughts flashed through her mind in an instant.

Not only had she previously shared his belief, but also in better times, they would sometimes make fun of Christians together. Should she, then, hide her "Steps to Christ[1]", or not? She felt as if she should, but for some reason beyond her understanding, she could not. It was as if her hands froze to its open page, her eyes fastened, as if stuck there. As he drew within a few steps of her, and she became aware of his proximity, fear took a hold of her. Hastily, she tried to put the book away. Too late! He had caught her.

"You're up early today", she smiled, putting on a brave face, trying to divert his attention.

Ignoring her comment, he asked, "What are you reading?"

Before she could answer, he continued, "You're all dressed up I see. Where are you going?"

"I'm going to church with Marissa", she replied, doing a master job of hiding her anxiety.

"You're going to church?"

"Yes", she replied, mustering up her courage.

---

[1] Ellen G. White, © 1892

AN ACT OF COMPASSION

What came next completely floored her.

"Well, you look *very* nice", he said. "Enjoy your day".

"Huh?" she thought, open-mouthed. "Oh, th-thank you!" she managed to utter at length, as he turned to make his way to the kitchen.

She could not remember the last time he had given her a compliment. As if that were not enough, he did not question her going to church, but instead, wished her a good day! That was the last thing she had expected. Still shocked, she returned her eyes to the page, but now found it difficult to concentrate on what she was reading. She continued staring at the words, with a pleased and puzzled expression on her face. Little was sinking in.

Returning from the kitchen and making his way upstairs, Matthew almost collided with Marissa coming out of her room, now having finally completed her grooming. Seeing her, Rebecca thought it was worth the wait. Wearing a pastel floral dress with a beige jacket and light beige shoes, her daughter looked the perfect picture of pristine beauty.

"Hi, Marissa!" he greeted her, before Rebecca had a chance to comment.

"Hi, Dad! Good morning!" Marissa replied, taken aback by his cheerful greeting.

"You look very nice!" he said, as he looked at her from head to toe.

"Oh, thanks Dad! Thank you!" she responded, stunned.

"Ready for church?" he asked approvingly.

"Sure am!" she beamed. His compliment was probably the most pleasant surprise she had ever had.

"Well, you ladies have a great day!" he said, as he made his way back upstairs, coffee in one hand, and the morning newspaper in the other. Rebecca and Marissa gazed at his retreating figure and then at each other in amazement. Each one knew exactly what the other was thinking.

"What just happened here?" Rebecca finally spoke.

"We must be dreaming", Marissa replied. "Let's

get out of here before we wake up". With that, they headed for the front door, their faces made radiant by the early morning sun and by the peace with which they had left their often-turbulent dwelling. The glare of the sun forced Marissa to put her sunglasses on, making her look "real cool", as Kezia later told her. It promised to be a lovely day.

Having no idea that on the evening of the pastor's visit, Matthew had heard and been greatly influenced by his words, they could not understand his reaction, or his general change of attitude. Matthew, on the other hand, had hid in his heart the words that he had heard. They had greatly softened his attitude toward God and religion, and were gradually changing his general outlook on life. As Marissa and Rebecca stepped out into the beautiful morning sun, the dew glistening on the well-manicured lawn, reflecting its soft rays, they felt content.

Matthew had always taken pride in his home. He made sure that he mowed the lawn and trimmed the hedges well. Even with his drinking, that was one thing he did not neglect. Beautiful flowers and shrubs, and a hedge that boasted the picture of perfection decorated the front yard. Inhaling deeply the lavender-perfumed air, Marissa thought of the goodness and power of God, as revealed in His creation.

She had learned in Bible class how God made the earth and all that it contains in six days. "Wow!" she thought. "How awesome is God! All the beautiful flowers, the different kinds of fruits and plants, the different kinds of birds and fish and animals, God made all of that and more in only six days! God is wonderful!" She knew her science teacher would not agree, but she believed the Bible, and it felt good to know that this great God, who created everything, loved her and wanted her to live with Him forever.

Before they drove off, Marissa, following the example of Kezia and her parents, offered to pray for God's protection on their journey. Rebecca was deeply moved by the humility and trust reflected in her daughter's simple prayer. Listening to a gospel

AN ACT OF COMPASSION

CD that Kezia had given to Marissa, they drove along the almost traffic-free Saturday-morning streets.

As they had intended, they arrived on time-- a little early, even. As usual, a warm welcome awaited them at the door. As they entered the sanctuary, a hush came over them. The melodious sound of the organist softly playing a song of devotion to God filled them with a sense of awe. The peace and tranquility of the atmosphere gave them the assurance that they were in the protective presence of a powerful, yet kind and loving God.

Matthew, in the meantime, read his newspaper distractedly. For some reason, he had a feeling of unrest that he could not explain. He was not going to go to the pub today. He did not feel like it. He wondered what it would be like to be in church. What would his wife and daughter be doing now? Becky seemed happy, even eager to go. It was nice seeing her and Marissa all dressed up. It was hard to believe, though, that she would even *think* of going to church. Well, good for them. That was not for him. Still, he could not forget the words of the pastor, and the impact it had on him. Turning to the sports page, he took a big gulp of his coffee. This time the scores did not interest him much. His mind was just not there.

He knew that something had happened to him on the night of the pastor's visit. He also knew that since then, a change had come over his wife, as well. She was happier than she had been in a long time, and so was their daughter. As for him, he knew that his changed outlook was no coincidence. He remembered how he felt when he heard the pastor's prayer. "There must be something to this God thing, after all; it's no use denying it", he concluded; "but I can't see myself going to church or getting involved in any of that religious stuff".

With a prolonged yawn, he glanced up from his newspaper, suddenly remembering that it was time to mow the lawn. As he was about to rise, his eyes caught sight of a book that his wife had left on the night table. It had been there for some time, but he had not noticed it before. Curiously, he picked it up.

"Hmm, that's interesting!" he thought. 'A New Beginning'! That's what *I* need".

After flipping through and looking at the title of each chapter, he turned back and read the introduction. It talked about a man who had come from a troubled home, wracked with abuse of every description. Drug and alcohol abuse, sexual abuse, physical and verbal abuse were some of the atrocities he had experienced in his youth. He had survived it all, and had become happy and peaceful in adulthood, leading a productive life, which he attributed to having given over his life to God's control.

Captivated by the story and wanting to know how that chapter would end, he forgot about the lawn for a moment and continued reading. In a short while, he had read the entire book. By this time, he was beginning to be convinced that there must be a God, and One who cares. This man's situation was clearly hopeless, yet his life turned around so dramatically. "Surely", he thought, "if God could deliver *him* from such a vice, why not me?" After all, his situation was not nearly as bad.

This man had never known security, love or happiness in his life, before he met Jesus Christ. That was not *his* situation. He had known all of these at some point in his life. This man had a near death encounter, and also spent time in prison for a vicious crime, where the gospel reached him. He had not had any such experience. If God could save *this* man, God could certainly save *him*.

In actuality, Matthew's situation paled in comparison to the protagonist of the short book, but he knew that, like this man, he needed rescue. How can I come to know God as *he* did? Jesus died so that anyone who chooses may receive salvation, he had read.

He had also overheard the pastor say those words. But how do I choose? he wondered. Do I just say, 'Jesus, I choose to be saved?' His musings continued. Even if it were that simple, would Jesus accept me, if I come to Him simply because I need to be delivered from my desperation?

Without thinking, he picked up the Bible that

AN ACT OF COMPASSION

was sitting beside the book he had just read. Rebecca had received that Bible as a gift at church. She took it to church with her every time she went, but for some strange reason she had forgotten to take it this time.

As he opened it, his eyes landed on Matthew 11:28. 'Come unto me, all ye that labour and are heavy laden, and I will give you rest'. It was as if God was speaking to him directly. In wonderment he stared at the page. This is saying that I can come to Jesus even if it is because I am burdened with a problem, and He will accept me!

This answers my question exactly! He looked at the verse repeatedly, and was about to close the Bible, still pondering what he had just read. Suddenly the thought came to him, "I should note this verse, so I can come back to it again later. It's like a message sent to me". Opening the drawer beside his bed and reaching for his diary, he jotted down the text under the date of its discovery.

Before closing the diary, he sketched a tiny light bulb beside his note, indicating that he had had an epiphany. Jesus had invited him to come and seek rest in Him. He took no thought at that time, that Jesus was offering rest, not only from the pressing problems that weighed so heavily upon him, but also, rest from the burden of his sin. He only knew that he was tired of the burdens he bore, and was ready to lay them down.

Feeling now a sense of hopefulness, he returned to his newspaper, intending to read just one more article before mowing the lawn. Before he could even finish a full paragraph, the doorbell rang. He could not be bothered with annoying sales people now; he thought, he would just ignore it and continue reading. Not a chance! The persistent ringing would not allow him to concentrate.

Could his wife and daughter have returned home already? Even if that were the case, which was unlikely, they each had a key. They would not be ringing the doorbell. He was just about to go down and give this nuisance a piece of his mind when suddenly, the ringing stopped. Ah! What a relief! He sat back down and again reached for his newspaper, but his peace was short-lived.

As soon as he opened the pages, the sound of an urgent knock pierced his ears. "What now!" he exclaimed, looking out the window onto the empty driveway. "Becky's car is not there", he muttered. "I knew they could not be back already". His car was out of sight, but it seemed someone knew he was at home and would not leave until he answered the door. It couldn't be any of the guys he hung out with at the pub. None of them lived in walking distance from his house. Jimmy lived the closest to his house, and he's so lazy, he'd never walk that far if you paid him. So who could it be? He wondered.

"I'd better get that door right away. That seems to be the only way I'll get rid of whoever is there, so I can get on with my day. Now I'm hungry too, come to think of it! I'll just deal with this real quick", he muttered.

As he came near, the knock came yet another time.

"Oh! For crying out loud! Who is it?" he shouted, making not the least attempt to conceal his annoyance.

"My name's Peter", said the first nuisance.

"And I'm Tyler", said the other.

"May we intrude on your time for just a minute, please?" Peter asked.

"You already have. What can I do for you?" He retorted.

"We're visiting with people in the neighborhood, and we felt impressed that the Lord wanted us to come to your house to share with you the gospel of Jesus Christ and His great love for you".

"Strange?" Matthew thought. "Was I not just reading something about that?" Still, he did not intend to entertain any discussion on the subject at this time. He did not want anyone preaching to him.

"Not right now, thank you!" he answered curtly through the closed door.

"We won't be long", Tyler persisted cautiously, "we have some information we would like to share with you that we believe you will be very happy to receive".

"I'm not interested, thank you!" he replied

brusquely. Matthew was not bending. Not only was he occupied and hungry, he was also vulnerable, and afraid he might yield. He now believed in the existence of God, and knew he needed Him, but no one was going to talk him into submission.

"Is there a more convenient time that we may call on you?" Peter asked gently.

"I don't think so!" he snapped.

"Is it okay then, if we leave you some literature?"

That was the ideal way of escape. He could handle that.

"Sure. Just leave it in the mailbox, thanks", he replied politely.

He wanted to know more about God, but he would do his own seeking in his own time and under his own terms. Having some material to read would suit him just fine. He picked up the tracts and saw the words 'Come Unto Me'. He looked at it curiously. "That's the identical thing I read earlier! What are the chances of *that* happening?" he wondered aloud. Putting aside his hunger and his work, he read it. The other tract had the title, "Seek ye the Lord", based on two major texts. The first was Jeremiah 29; 11-13. It said:

For I know the thoughts that I think toward you saith the Lord, thoughts of peace and not of evil, to give you an expected end. Then ye shall call upon me, and ye shall go and pray unto me, and I will hearken unto you. And ye shall seek me, and find me, when ye shall search for me with all your heart.

The second text, Isaiah 55:6, said, **'Seek ye the Lord while He may be found. Call upon Him while He is near'.** Instead of heading for the kitchen, as intended, he went back upstairs and secured the tracts in the drawer with his diary. Convinced that these occurrences were not merely coincidental, but that they were arranged by divine providence, he made a decision. He *would* seek the Lord. From then on, he read the Bible secretly.

SEVEN

WHO IS THAT MAN?

Some time had gone by since Matthew started reading the Bible. His wife continued to notice increasingly greater positive changes in him, which continued to baffle her. Marissa also found him easier to be around. In addition to not losing his temper nearly as often, he seemed a lot more energetic and cheerful. Abuse toward them had now become non-existent.

Of course, they did not have a lot of money, so that could have accounted for his reduced alcohol intake, Rebecca reasoned: but what about his demeanor? She could not figure *that* out. She cherished that surprise compliment he had given her when he first discovered that she was going to church, but his attitude was not just the result of a temporary upswing in his mood, as she had first thought. What caused the change? That was the big puzzle. Recognizing the futility in her attempts to solve this mystery, she concluded, "I'm not complaining; whatever the reason, I'll take it".

While Rebecca wondered about Matthew's reduced interest in his favorite brand of beer, little did she know that something else was brewing. She and Marissa awoke earlier than usual one Saturday morning as the fall approached, and started getting ready for church. They wanted to arrive before the expected throng of visitors for a special program conducted by a visiting evangelist. Although they would be willing to give up their seats to the newer visitors, they desired to have a choice seat in the House for the beginning of the event, if possible. As Marissa helped her Mom with her hair, she noticed from the bathroom window, a tall, well-dressed man standing beside the car in the driveway.

"Who is that man?" she asked.

"It looks like Pastor Pottinger", her Mom replied, standing up so she could have a better view. They wondered why the pastor had come to visit so early in the morning.

"Could there be a change in the program?" Marissa wondered aloud.

"No, I don't think so. That would only happen if a hurricane came overnight and blew down the building", her Mom chuckled.

"That's right!" Marissa smiled. "All kidding aside though, only some big emergency could prevent that event from going ahead. Let's hope nothing happened".

"Yes, let's hope", her Mom agreed.

"If something *did* happen, the pastor could not possibly make personal visits to everyone, nor would he need to. There would be people assigned to pass the information around", Marissa reasoned.

"Well, I guess we'll find out soon enough why he's here", her Mom concluded.

"I hope he doesn't knock before I finish with your hair. I finally got it in the right grip and I wouldn't want to have to let go of it. I'd have to start all over again. By the way Mom, your hair looks beautiful in an upsweep, but maybe you could lighten it a bit. It's a lot of hair".

"You're right. Maybe I will", her Mom agreed.

"Do you think Dad would hear if the pastor should ring now?" Marissa asked, a bit concerned, knowing how grumpy her Dad gets if his sleep is disturbed.

"I don't think so. You know how soundly he sleeps", her Mom replied.

"Yes, I know, but if someone wakes him before he's ready, he's not a pretty fella". Marissa joked.

"You can say that again!" her Mom laughed.

"The pastor's not knocking", she added after a few minutes.

"No, he isn't! It looks as if he's tying his shoelace now". Marissa observed.

"Well, let's try and hurry out before he *does* knock".

"Okay, I'm done!" Marissa smiled, putting the comb back in its place. "Let's go".

"Remind me to park in the garage tonight when we get home". Rebecca said to Marissa, as they headed to the front door. "Those crab apples are starting to be a real headache. I'd rather not have to clean them off the windshield if I can avoid it".

"How can you park in the garage, Mom? There's no space left there for your car. Besides his car, Dad has everything there but his closet! Even the kitchen sink is there".

"Yeah, that's right! Our old kitchen sink is still there", her Mom recalled with a chuckle. "He thought maybe he would find some use for it someday. I think he knows now it has to go".

"Wait a minute, Mom! How did Pastor get here? Where's his car?" Marissa asked as they stepped out the door.

"You're right! His car is nowhere around. That's strange!"

As they came closer to the car, the man turned his head. Marissa gasped in surprise, while Rebecca just stared at him, speechless. Neither could believe her eyes. Matthew McBride had not put on a suit since his elder daughter got married five years ago. He had kept the suit he wore to her wedding for a special occasion—another wedding, perhaps. It was his only suit, and he looked dazzlingly handsome in it. Rebecca had forgotten that he even had that suit. It was all coming together now. *Now* they understood the mystery haircut he had gotten earlier in the week. They had complimented him on his new look, but had not a clue as to the reason behind it.

Many months had passed since he last saw the barber. They were happy to see him resembling his old self again, but had no idea that his motive went far beyond that. He did not want merely to be his old self again. He was on his way to becoming a new man. As Marissa and her Mom looked at him in pleasant wonderment, Matthew surprised them even further.

"What are you standing there staring at, you two? You don't want to be late for church, do you?" he asked with a whimsical smile, nudging Marissa good-humoredly, as he opened the door for her.

"N-No, we don't". Marissa stuttered, as she settled herself in the back seat. After closing her door, he opened the front passenger door for his

AN ACT OF COMPASSION

wife, and closed it as she sat. He then took his place in the driver's seat. Rebecca had no words. She could only muster a pleasantly puzzled stare at him, as they fastened their seatbelts.

"Let's go then!" he said jovially, leaving Marissa and Rebecca stupefied. "Where is the church, anyway?" he asked his still stunned wife. Shaking herself out of the shock, she gave him the directions. Silence and serenity accompanied them all the way to the quaint little church. As they entered the building, the members met them with an avalanche of warm embraces and handshakes.

They were particularly thrilled to meet Marissa's father. Mrs. McBride glowed as she saw her husband shaking hands and exchanging greetings. He had not put on a pleasant smile for quite some time, until recently. Now he seemed radiant. That was sheer joy for Rebecca, but nothing could compare to his actual presence there, with her and their daughter. She would never have dreamed of that happening—not in a million years! Until recently, she could never have pictured herself in

WHO IS THAT MAN?

church, much less being there with her husband! Simultaneously she felt a peace and an excitement that seemed almost unreal.

The initial awkwardness Matthew felt, having refused to meet with the pastor when he visited their home, quickly disappeared. Of course, the pastor had no knowledge of Matthew's reaction to the news of his coming to their home; but Matthew could not help feeling a sense of guilt for his behavior. The hospitality of the members, and the pastor's welcoming embrace, reassured him that he had no cause for concern.

Greetings over, they took their seats in preparation for the morning Bible study session. As the session began, Matthew listened with intent, but did not speak. His wife, on the other hand, had a burning question for which she urgently needed an answer. Now familiar with the environment, and encouraged by the easy manner of the teacher, she felt confident to voice her question. The presence of her husband sitting beside her also seemed to have increased her confidence. When the teacher asked if

AN ACT OF COMPASSION

anyone wanted to share a testimony that might encourage others in their walk with God, many testified of His guiding hand in the experiences they had encountered during the week.

"I don't have a testimony to share, but I have what you might call a burning question".

"Okay. Let's see if we can help", the teacher smiled invitingly.

"I told a friend of mine, my coworker, about visiting your church, and learning about the Bible. She said something that left me baffled. I didn't know how to respond, and it's been gnawing at me ever since".

"What did she say?" the teacher asked.

"She said that there is no particular day of rest, it is a matter of choice. She also said that God did not create the world in six *literal* days, but in different time spans, each of which could have spread over thousands or even millions of years. Could that be true?"

"That's definitely a question for our afternoon Bible study session, but we wouldn't want to leave you hanging, so let's see what we can do now to address it briefly here. Turn with me to the book of Genesis Chapter 1 and let us see what the Bible says. Would you please read verses 1-5 for us?"

From the King James Version she read:

In the beginning God created the heaven and the earth.
And the earth was without form, and void; and darkness was upon the face of the deep. And the Spirit of God moved upon the face of the waters.
And God said, Let there be light: and there was light.
And God saw the light, that it was good: and God divided the light from the darkness.
And God called the light Day, and the darkness he called Night. And the evening and the morning were the first day.

"Thank you. Let's focus on that last sentence. *'And the evening and the morning were the first day'*. You will have noticed that the 'day' to which the Bible refers consists of an evening and a morning, right?"

"Yes, I noticed that".

"How do you understand that sentence?"

"I'm not sure".

"Would you agree that one evening and one morning is contained in a twenty- four hour time period, which is one literal day?"

"Yes, I would".

"Actually, a full day starts at evening and ends at evening. In Leviticus 23: 32, we are told that the Sabbath is to be celebrated from evening to evening, which means from sunset to sunset. If we had time to read this entire chapter, we would find that God created everything in six days, each consisting of an evening and a morning. Genesis 2: 2 says that God rested on the seventh day from all His work, and in Exodus 20, He reminded His people of the significance of that day. Let's turn to Exodus Chapter 20 verses 8 to 11 and see what it says".

From the King James Version, she read:

Remember the Sabbath day, to keep it holy.
Six days shalt thou labor, and do all thy work:

> **But the seventh day is the sabbath of the LORD thy God: in it thou shalt not do any work, thou, nor thy son, nor thy daughter, thy manservant, nor thy maidservant, nor thy cattle, nor thy stranger that is within thy gates:**
>
> **For in six days the LORD made heaven and earth, the sea, and all that in them is, and rested the seventh day: wherefore the LORD blessed the sabbath day, and hallowed it.**

"Thank you. Any questions on what you've just read?"

"Oh, no, it's quite clear! It says that we should do all our work in six days, and keep the seventh day holy, because the Lord created everything in six days and rested the seventh", she replied.

"Excellent! God would not require us to do anything that we could not possibly do. Since no human being has ever lived for even *one* thousand years, it would be impossible to keep the Sabbath holy, as God commanded, if the days of creation were time periods consisting of thousands, or even millions of years instead of literal days. So according to the Bible, we can safely conclude that the Sabbath is a specific day consisting of 24 hours like all the other six days. Does that answer your question?"

"It answers my question perfectly".

"Wonderful! Feel free to share with us in the future, any other questions you may have".

"Actually, I have another very important question on my mind at this time, but I will leave it for another time".

"Your previous question was so interesting, I'm anxious to hear this one also, even if we cannot answer it now, so go ahead.

"Do we have any proof that Saturday is the seventh day of the week as God gave it? I have heard it said that the calendar has been changed, so we can't really be sure"

"Oh, that's another great question, but, you are right. We will have to leave it for the afternoon session. We will be better able to address it then. It will take some time to do it justice".

"I can't wait to hear what the answer will be", Rebecca thought.

WHO IS THAT MAN?

"Thank you for that question. We can look forward to a lively discussion on that topic later. Now, we have a very exciting topic for our lesson study this week. Let us repeat the memory verse.

In unison the class repeated 2 Corinthians 5: 17 **"Therefore if any man be in Christ, he is a new creature: old things are passed away; behold, all things are become new"**. That appealed to Matthew. He quietly absorbed as much as his mind could process from the spirited discussion that followed. When the class ended, he felt like a child who had just finished the last bite of his favorite treat. He enjoyed it while it lasted, but wished there were more.

"Regrettably, we have come to the end of our discussion", the moderator commented. "It has been wonderful! Join us again next Sabbath morning for another stimulating session. God bless you as you continue to worship Him", she said in conclusion.

"Amen!" the group responded, as the morning Bible session ended, and the next session began.

EIGHT

ALMOST UNREAL

Questions raced through Matthew's mind, as he listened attentively, absorbing all that he heard and saw. Marissa, sitting beside her parents, found it a bit difficult to concentrate on anything else. The thought of having them in church with her, especially her Dad, occupied her mind almost totally. Ever since she came to know about God, she had been praying that God would reveal Himself to him. Now it seemed as if her prayers were being answered beyond her expectation.

Her greatest delight came from observing the interest with which he listened to the word of God. It was almost unreal. She savored every moment. Being interested in the things of God would make him even a better Dad than he was before his troubles began. That thought filled her with excitement. She knew the peace that she enjoyed by learning about Jesus in the Bible study group. Her Mom was about to join that group. Now it seemed a real possibility that she could be in Bible class with both her parents! How cool was *that*!

Usually easily bored, Matthew had not a dull moment being in church. He totally immersed himself in the environment that until a few moments ago was foreign to him. Rebecca's thoughts went back and forth between the thrill of being in church with her family, and the words of the speaker on the podium.

Before long, the voice of the elder inviting to the altar those who desired to have special prayers jolted her and Marissa from their respective pleasant musings. "Cast all your cares upon Him, for He cares for you", the elder echoed the call of the apostle Peter in 1 Peter 5: 7, as he extended the invitation to the congregation to lay their burdens at the feet of Jesus, while he interceded on their behalf.

Matthew trembled. He wanted to respond, but lacked the courage to make the move. More than anything else, he wanted deliverance, but feared surrendering the control of his will to a power outside of himself. Although the elder did not direct his appeal at this time to those who wanted to accept Christ as their Savior, Matthew felt that in order to receive the Lord's deliverance, he would have to submit to His will. He knew he needed to. He wanted to, but he dreaded it.

What would he have to give up if he chose to follow Jesus all the way? Was he ready? Was he capable? Was he good enough? Yet he yearned for healing in his life. He was torn. He had already made tremendous progress toward being free from alcohol addiction. He knew that it was the working of God. He wanted complete deliverance in that area, and in all other aspects of his life.

The word of God that had lodged in his heart had already resulted in considerable positive changes in his life, as evidenced by the fact that he was sitting in a church pew beside his wife and daughter. Why then was he hesitating when he knew what he had to do? While he contemplated, Kezia rose up. Marissa followed. Then Kezia's parents started moving out of the pew. Before the prayer began, Marissa looked down at her Dad and sensed his conflict. Walking back to their seat, she took his hand in one hand and her Mom's in the other, and together they walked to the altar.

Tranquility seemed to have wrapped itself around the Mc Bride family at that moment. Matthew experienced a sensation of comfort akin to the embrace of a warm blanket on the body of a runaway on a cold winter's night. The family felt closer to each other than ever before.

As the elder prayed, Matthew fought with futility to contain the tears that now flowed copiously down his face. He soon discarded any thought of embarrassment and surrendered to sweet release, as the elder prayed for deliverance for those confronted with various perplexities. Every teardrop seemed to have had a cathartic effect on him, purifying him from all the pent-up debris that had clogged the pipeline of his life for so many years. The prayer seemed to him as if it were directed to God on *his*

AN ACT OF COMPASSION

behalf, regarding *his* particular issues. Believing that God had heard and would answer that prayer, he felt a profound sense of peace.

He left the altar feeling lighter, seeing the future brighter--a new man. He had unloaded his heart of a great burden and placed it at the feet of Jesus. He felt as if a brilliant light had broken in upon the thick darkness of his soul. Now more than ever, he wanted to know how to become a follower of Christ.

His opportunity came sooner than imagined. Shortly after the elder's prayer, and a medley of soul-stirring musical renditions of praise, adoration and supplication to God, the pastor took the pulpit.

There, a sermon undoubtedly transmitted from the very mind of God proceeded from his lips. It depicted the great redeeming love of God for humankind, His desire to shield and to defend, to provide for and to protect, and ultimately, to save. It spoke to Matthew, answering all the questions that had puzzled him. Again, he felt as if the speaker was addressing him directly, conveying to him a message from the Lord.

Following the sermon was a solemn song of appeal, during the singing of which, the pastor invited all who desired to submit their lives to Christ to come forward. This time, Matthew did not hesitate. His moment had come. He needed no prompting and no company.

Tossing aside all inhibitions, he walked to the altar alone. His wife joined him, taking his hand. Marissa followed. Matthew felt the awesome presence of God, as he stood there. The pastor prayed thanking God for the leading of His Holy Spirit that had touched the hearts of those who responded, and asking for His continued guidance in their lives, and for their full surrender to the healing, cleansing power of Jesus Christ.

After this, the elder gave a card to all respondents to complete, indicating their desired spiritual support. The Mc Brides requested Bible study in their home.

After the service, the Lafontaines offered to give spiritual support to the family in whatever way they needed it, and so did many others. The head deacon

AN ACT OF COMPASSION

invited them to join his family for lunch. Still tired from the double shift she had completed the previous day, Rebecca politely declined, choosing instead to go home. She wanted to have a nap, so she could return refreshed and alert for the afternoon session, where she would receive the answer to the question she had asked during the morning Bible study class.

Matthew and Marissa stayed and had lunch with the Bradbury family. With their two teen-aged daughters and a young adult son, they had a sumptuous meal, after which, they engaged in a lively Bible game, joined by Kezia.

Everyone knew Kezia Lafontaine and Jonathan Bradbury to be the ones to beat at that game, so they each teamed up with one of the Bradbury twin, Bethany and Tiffany. Their knowledge of the Bible so greatly impressed Marissa and her Dad, as they watched them play, that they wanted to have a copy of that game for their own family. After the game, the group became engaged in an enthusiastic Bible discussion. As before, Matthew listened quietly.

ALMOST UNREAL

Rebecca, in the meantime, on her way home, thought about her question and wondered what the answer would be. She could hardly wait to hear it. She now knew that the six days of creation were literal days. If she could show biblical proof that the day the calendar now shows as Saturday was the same day that God had blessed all those years of long ago, she could deal with any opposition she would encounter from Priscilla.

More importantly, she wanted to be able to confirm by the Holy Bible that this group of people was truly teaching and walking according to the will and the word of God. She wanted to be sure that she was not becoming involved in a cult, according to what she had heard about this group. It promised to be a very interesting evening, which filled her with anticipation. Her excitement grew, as she continued on her journey.

While the lunchtime crowd engaged in Bible games and discussions, Elder and Mrs. Gibson made their way to the hospital to visit. Both staff and patients looked forward to their visits, which had lifted the spirits of everyone for many years. The Gibsons, on the other hand, derived great satisfaction from the knowledge that their presence made a difference. They had faithfully carried out this ministry and looked forward to continuing it for many years to come. The satisfaction it gave them seemed to increase with each visit.

On their way back, Elder Gibson thought about Rebecca's question, sorting out in his mind the texts he would use to answer it. He anticipated a stimulating discussion, and was eager to get it under way.

Usually, whenever they returned from their hospital visits, they would find people sitting quietly, perhaps reading, or conversing about scripture, the lesson study or some other biblical subject matter. Today, they returned to find a spirited discussion on end time prophecy. It held everyone captivated. Rebecca had arrived a few minutes before the Gibsons, and caught the last bit of the discussion. This whetted her appetite for more.

As the discussion continued, Elder Gibson, realizing that this topic, being of such great interest, could easily preempt the Bible class, knew he had to intervene. Reluctantly, he announced:

"Good afternoon and happy Sabbath to everyone! It is always encouraging to see a discussion on end time prophecy with such enthusiasm, especially when the young people are involved. There is no doubt that we are living in the last days of earth's history. I hope to join you in this discussion at another time. Unfortunately, though, at this time, I must interrupt, as it is now time for our regular Bible class. I invite you all to participate, and make it as lively as the discussion you have been having. So, without further ado, we will now begin our Bible class, as we are a bit behind".

As soon as she heard the announcement, Rebecca made her way to the front. This was her moment. She wanted to hear everything. Ever since she started attending church, Priscilla had been trying to convince her that only misguided people, still living in the 'Old Dispensation', kept the

Sabbath. She described Sabbath keepers as cult followers and legalists, living way behind the times.

Rebecca had thought at one point that Priscilla might be right, but shortly after she started visiting, she was convinced otherwise. Now she would have the information she needed in order to respond confidently to any objection her friend might raise regarding the validity of the Sabbath. Even more importantly, she would be able to fortify her own conviction that these people were indeed walking in the way of the Lord and abiding by the teachings of the Bible.

The elder began:

"I am happy to see so many of you here today. I would like to welcome you all. Again, happy Sabbath".

"Happy Sabbath!" the class resounded.

"Today, we will take a slightly different approach from our usual format. There will be no set topic of discussion. Instead, we will make it an open forum. This will allow anyone to ask any question they may have concerning the word of God, and together we will search the Scriptures to arrive at the answers.

Sister Gibson will display each question on the screen, so that those who might be joining us later will know what we discussed prior to their arrival. As we address each question, Sister Gibson will write below it the Bible text that answers it. What we cannot cover today, we will leave for the next session.

Bibles are available for anyone who needs one. If you do, just raise your hand and we will provide you with a Bible for your use in this session. Before we begin, let's pray".

Elder Gibson prayed that the Holy Spirit would lead them into all truth, and that God would open their minds to grasp and to retain what they were about to study. Then, much to Rebecca's delight, he said,

"This morning in our lesson study, Rebecca raised a very interesting question. As time did not permit us to answer it then, we deferred it to this session. So Rebecca, would you repeat your

AN ACT OF COMPASSION

question, please, for the benefit of those who were not present in our group this morning?"

"Certainly! How do we know for sure which day is the seventh day of the week?"

"Thank you. That's a very interesting question, isn't it?"

Heads nodded in agreement.

"Does anyone have a thought on that?"

"According to the calendar, Saturday is the seventh day of the week", Jonathan volunteered.

"That's very true. Although that is not the case with all calendars, our calendar *does* show Saturday as the seventh day. Thank you, Jonathan, for that answer. Are there any other insights?" the teacher asked.

"I would like to comment on that", Kezia's Mom offered.

"Thank you, Sister Lafontaine, go ahead please".

"The Bible provides clear proof that Saturday is the Sabbath".

"I agree. Share with us how".

"I encounter this question very frequently in my

witnessing experience, so I have the supporting texts readily available. Give me a moment to get my notes".

"Certainly!" The teacher waited, as she opened her briefcase.

"The texts to which I refer in answering that question are: **Matthew 27 and 28, Mark 15 and 16, Luke 23 and 24, John 19 and 20.** We learn from Mark 15: 42, Luke 23: 54 and John 19: 41, 42 that Jesus' crucifixion and burial took place on the Preparation Day, specified as the day before the Sabbath. Luke 23:56 tells us that after His crucifixion, the women who had accompanied Him on His journey returned home and prepared spices and ointments and rested on the Sabbath day, **according to the commandment**. They returned to the sepulcher the day after the Sabbath, which was the first day of the week, the day on which Jesus rose from the dead, as Luke 24: 1-6 tells us.

"The Bible plainly states that the day after the Sabbath was the first day of the week. It is common knowledge that Jesus rose from the dead on a

AN ACT OF COMPASSION

Sunday morning, which means that Sunday is the first day of the week. The day before Sunday on any calendar is Saturday. Since the week has seven days, the day that comes before the first must be the seventh. That makes it clear to me that the day we call Saturday is the Sabbath day, to put it in a nutshell".

"Thank you, Sister Lafontaine. Very well put. It is wonderful that you had the references handy, and thank you for answering the question so succinctly. I believe that this question concerns many, so we would like to ensure that everyone understands the answer perfectly. Let us explore it a little further.

"Jesus was crucified the day before the Sabbath. Luke 23: 54 says, 'that day was the preparation [day], and the Sabbath drew on'. He rose from the dead the day after the Sabbath. Matthew 28: 1, 2 tells us that that was the first day of the week. I have been confronted with this question myself. Some claim that since the word Saturday is not in the Bible, we cannot know if the day that God called the Sabbath is the day we now know as Saturday. So, let's work through this a bit. How many days are in the week?"

"Seven!" The answer came in chorus.

"What is the name that we call the first day of the week?"

"Sunday!" the class again chorused.

"And what is the name of the day that comes immediately before Sunday on all calendars?"

"Saturday!"

"One of my friends gave me a Chinese calendar, which shows Monday as the first day of the week, but even on that calendar, Saturday is the day that comes before Sunday", Tiffany offered.

"Very true! Even in those calendars that focus only on the workweek, Saturday is still the day that comes before Sunday. So, as we mentioned earlier, Matthew 28: 1, 2 shows that the Sabbath is the day that comes immediately before the first day of the week. Since the week has seven days, the day that comes before the first day must be the seventh, as Sister Lafontaine pointed out. And as we have established, that day is Saturday. Is that clear to everyone?"

"It's clear!" the class responded.

"Let me see if I can put it all together", Rebecca offered, wanting to make sure she got it right. "The Bible says that the Sabbath is the day that comes right after the Crucifixion and right before the Resurrection. Since childhood, I have understood that Friday was the day of the Crucifixion and Sunday the day of the Resurrection. The day that comes right after Friday and right before Sunday, is Saturday. So, although the Bible does not use the word Saturday, the information that it gives us, along with what we know from the calendar, leaves no doubt in my mind that the day we know as Saturday is the seventh day, the Sabbath of the Lord. That is the day that the Lord blessed and commands us to keep holy".

"Precisely! You aced it! You are now ready to share that information confidently with *anyone*, and I hope you do. We will not go into all the other texts at this time, but there are a couple that I especially want you to remember. **Matthew 28: 1, 2**. Rebecca, when you find it, would you read it for us, please?"

From the King James Version she read:

In the end of the Sabbath as it began to dawn toward the first day of the week, came Mary Magdalene and the other Mary to see the sepulcher..."

"Good. That text alone provides irrefutable proof of the Sabbath day". Take special note also of **Luke 23: 54-56.** You can easily remember these two.

"Thank you, that is very helpful. There is one other thing Priscilla said that puzzles me though, if I may", Rebecca continued.

"You certainly may, Rebecca. Let's hear it", the teacher smiled.

"She said that the calendar has undergone changes over the years, since God gave the Ten Commandments, which makes it impossible for us to know which day He really commanded us to keep. Could it be that the first day of the week we just read about in the Bible was a different day from the one we know today?"

"Well, let's see. According to the book of

AN ACT OF COMPASSION

Genesis, as we learned earlier, the world began with a seven-day week. That has not changed. There have been changes in the calendar, which we will not delve into at this time, but evidently, those changes did not affect the number or the order of the days of the week. However, there is a sure way of telling whether or not there has been a change in the order of the days. Do you remember to which nation God originally give the Ten Commandments?"

"He gave them to the Children of Israel!" Kezia answered.

"That's right! God spoke them directly to the Children of Israel, commonly known today as the Jews. (By the way, although we loosely refer to the Children of Israel as Jews, not all of the Children of Israel are Jews. Strictly speaking, the Jews are descendants of Judah). God instructed the Children of Israel to teach the Commandments to their children and to their children's children, and to pass them on to the other nations of the world.

Although they were not always faithful in keeping the commandments, the observance of the

Sabbath has been handed down unchanged from the time God gave them to Moses at Mount Sinai to this present generation. And what day do the Jews observe as God's holy day?"

"Now I understand. I know many Jewish people, who do not work on Saturdays. They even close their businesses for a part of the day on Fridays. Now I get it! That's because Friday is the Preparation Day. That's why I always thought of Saturday as the Jewish Sabbath", Rebecca reflected.

"And you are not alone! That is a common misconception. It is important to note that God Himself numbered the days of the week at creation, and blessed the seventh day. At that time there were no Jews. He gave the Sabbath to humankind, as a memorial of His creation. God did not give the commandments--including the Sabbath--to the Jews, for themselves alone, but to be taken to the entire world. What God puts in place, He does not change. He says in Malachi 3: 6, 'I am the Lord, I change not'. Does that answer your question?"

"That clears up everything for me. Thank you!"

NINE

A REAL EYE-OPENER

The questions that Rebecca asked led to many others. Elder Gibson received them gladly. Seeing the raised hand of a familiar visitor, he asked, "Mr. Kennedy, Do you have a question for us?"

"Yes, my granddaughter Kayla has been attending your Vacation Bible School for the past two summers. She's graduating later this afternoon, but I had a little extra time on my hands, so I came early".

"Thank you for joining our class. How has Kayla been enjoying her time at Vacation Bible School?"

"Oh, she loves it! She has been having a great time and learning a lot. She comes home and talks about the things she sees on her nature walks, and the things she learns about Jesus. She brings home crafts that she makes. She even learned about healthy eating and tries to do a bit of cooking. She shows us some of the exercises she has learned and we do them together. It's a great way for the kids to occupy themselves in the summer time. I am really happy she had that opportunity".

"That's wonderful!" Elder Gibson responded.

"I understand your explanation about the Sabbath, but do you really think that it matters that much to God *when* we rest? I have to tell you, there's a lot that I like about your organization, but I can't help wondering if you might not be making too big a deal about this Sabbath thing".

"Thank you for sharing that concern, Mr. Kennedy", Elder Gibson responded. "We base our observance of the Lord's Sabbath, not on our opinion, but on His word. You might want to read it for yourself in Exodus 20, verses 8-10".

"The Sabbath is a commemoration of God's creation. When we observe it, we are acknowledging God as our Creator and Sovereign Lord. In Ezekiel 20: 20, He says, 'Hallow my Sabbaths, and they shall be a sign between me and you, that you may know that I am the Lord your God. The Sabbath is probably the greatest test of loyalty humankind has ever had since that of Adam and Eve in the Garden of Eden. It matters to God what day we rest; He commands us to observe the day that He has blessed. By our observance of the Sabbath, we indicate that we have chosen *His* way, rather than the tradition of men. A seemingly insignificant act of disobedience brought sin into the world, remember? God forbade one particular tree; he sanctified one particular day".

"You have a point there", Mr. Kennedy agreed. "That's really something to think about".

"I have a question!" A voice came from the back.

"Good! What's your question, Marissa?" the teacher invited.

"If people do everything else that God commands, but do not keep the Sabbath, will that keep them from going to heaven when Jesus returns?" Marissa asked.

"That's a very interesting question! Would

anyone like to comment?" the teacher asked.

An eager hand went up. It was that of Justin, another visitor. It seems as if he could not wait to answer Marissa's question.

"I don't know", he said, "but if ever I've seen a man of God it's Reverend Haughton. He is the kindest, most compassionate person I know! He's always ready to give a helping hand and an encouraging word. He even helped us with food and stuff when my Dad was out of work. He's a real good person. He does everything right, as far as I'm concerned, but he says Sunday is the day we should keep holy in honor of Jesus' resurrection. He says that Jesus came to earth to bring us grace and truth, and that we are living in the dispensation of grace. I'm sure God would not keep a man like *that* out of heaven just for not keeping Saturday holy".

"That's very interesting. If I understand you correctly, you believe that God will reward Reverend Haughton with a place in heaven for his good works, and for his good character, even if he does not obey all of God's commandments. Did I

AN ACT OF COMPASSION

sum it up correctly?" the teacher asked.

"You sure did!" Justin responded.

"Let's see what the Bible says. Revelation 22:14 is one of the many texts that could answer that question. Would you please read that for us, Justin?"

"Sure! It says, 'Blessed are they that do His commandments that they may have right to the tree of life, and may enter in through the gates into the city".

"Thank you very much. What do you understand from that verse?"

"Okay, I think it means that we must obey all of God's commandments, if we want to enter into those pearly gates", Justin concluded.

"That's right. That's the way I understand it", the teacher replied.

"Elder Gibson, can you take one more question on this topic?" another visitor asked.

"I'd be happy to. This topic is very important. If we have to devote the whole session to it, that is what we will do. Please, go ahead!"

"My name is George. I am also here for the

Vacation Bible School graduation. My little brother is graduating today".

"Wonderful! Congratulations!"

"I have always understood that, according to the Scriptures, whoever keeps the law has fallen from grace. I actually saw it in the Bible somewhere, but I cannot recall where, at this time. How do you explain that?"

"You might be referring to Galatians 5: 4".

"Yes, that sounds like it".

"Thank you for raising that point. Let's go to Galatians 5:4. George, would you read that for us, please, when you find it?"

From the King James Version, George read, "'Christ is become of no effect unto you, whosoever of you is justified by the law; ye are fallen from grace'".

"Thank you. Now let us go to Ephesians 2:8. Whoever finds it first, please read".

Kezia read from the King James Version:

"'For by grace are ye saved through faith; and that not of yourselves: it is the gift of God'".

AN ACT OF COMPASSION

"Thank you, Kezia. Here we see that we are saved by grace through faith. It is not by our own merits, it is the gift of God. Let's go now to Romans 3:20. Marissa, I see your hand is up. Please read for us".

"Therefore by the deeds of the law there shall no flesh be justified in his sight: for by the law is the knowledge of sin", she read.

"Thank you. We see here that the law does not justify us; neither can it save us from our sins. It gives us the knowledge of sin. Nevertheless we cannot inhabit a sinless heaven and live forever with a holy God, without obeying His law, as we just read in Revelation 22: 14", the teacher explained.

"That seems reasonable, but there is also a text somewhere in the Bible that says we are not under the law. What does that mean?" George asked.

"You are probably referring to Romans 6:14, which says 'sin shall not have dominion over you, for ye are not under law, but under grace'. Is that the text you had in mind?"

"Yes, I think so".

A REAL EYE OPENER

"You are no doubt familiar with the expression, 'the long arm of the law'. That long arm reaches and subdues those who do not abide by the law. When we keep the law, we are not under its condemnation, which robs us of our freedom. In comparison, James 1: 25 speaks of God's law as the law of liberty, which will bring us blessings, if we abide by them. When we accept salvation, which is made available to us only by the grace of God through faith in Jesus Christ, we delight in keeping His law, because we love him, and the greatest manifestation of love is the desire to please. 1 John 5: 3 says, 'For this is the love of God that we keep his commandments: and his commandments are not grievous'. God's law does not enslave, it liberates. When we keep it, we are free from being under it.

"We know from Romans 3: 31 that the apostle Paul is not saying that being saved by grace through faith invalidates the law: There he asks this rhetorical question: 'Do we then make void the law through faith? God forbid: yea, we establish the law.' In Romans 6: 1, 2, he again asks rhetorically,

AN ACT OF COMPASSION

'What shall we say then, **shall we continue in sin that grace may abound**? God forbid!' And what is sin?"

"Doing what is wrong", George answered.

"That is right. What is the definition of sin, according to the Bible? Anyone?"

"According to the Bible in 1 John 3:4, 'Sin is the transgression of the law'", a voice spoke up.

"Thank you, Elder Lafontaine! You`ve been very quiet, but you're wide awake, I see!" Elder Gibson smiled.

"I sure am!" Elder Lafontaine chucked.

"Sin is the transgression of the law, so the law could never be done away with. Where there is no law there is no transgression, as we learn in Romans 4: 15. If there were no laws there would be no measure of right and wrong. That would lead to utter chaos. Anything would be permissible", Elder Gibson explained.

"That's right. The Moral Law stands forever. It is an indicator of our sinful nature and our need for grace", Brother Evans added.

Katherine, another visitor spoke up. "*My* pastor also says that anyone who thinks the law is still valid has fallen from grace. He has been a pastor for more than 35 years, and has a PhD in theology. Is he also mistaken?"

"When your pastor says that the law is done away with, referring to the Ten Commandments, is he mistaken? In a word, yes", Elder Gibson affirmed. "Think of it. If the Ten Commandments were done away with, it would be okay to steal, kill, dishonor your parents, commit adultery, or break any of the other laws which govern civilized society. Would you agree that your pastor would never think it acceptable to do any of those things?"

"I would definitely agree".

"Do you think then, that your pastor really means that the Moral Law, the Ten Commandments, is done away with, or is it more likely that he is referring only to a particular section of that law?" the teacher asked.

"That's an interesting question", Katherine replied pensively. "Now that I think about it, it doesn't seem as if Pastor Kent could really believe that the Ten Commandment law is done away with. I hate to admit it, but it seems as if that claim is only an excuse to reject the Sabbath", Katherine replied to the surprise of everyone, especially herself.

"I would not argue with that. Your pastor would probably not be happy to hear your conclusion, but truth is truth and when it confronts us, we cannot deny it. I am happy that you deduced that all on your own. It shows that you are open to the clear truth of the word of God", Elder Gibson smiled.

"There is one other concern regarding the Sabbath, though, that I need to voice", Katherine continued. "Does the Bible not say somewhere, that we should discontinue the reading of the Old Testament? I might not be stating it accurately, but you probably know the text to which I am referring".

"Yes, 2 Corinthians 3: 14 comes to mind. Let's find it together and see exactly what it says".

After a brief moment, several hands went up, having found the text. "Thank you all", the teacher smiled. "Katherine, would you read that verse for us, please?"

"Sure!" From the King James Version she read, 'But their minds were blinded: for until this day remaineth the same vail [veil] untaken away in the reading of the old testament; which vail [veil] is done away in Christ' ".

"Thank you. Is that the text you had in mind?"

"Yes, it is".

"If we had the time to read it all, we would see that earlier in the chapter, the writer makes reference to the veil with which Moses covered his face when he returned from the mount of God with the Ten Commandments. At that time, Moses' face shone so brightly from being in the presence of God that the people could not look upon his face, so when he spoke to them, he covered his face with a veil[1]. Also, at the crucifixion of Christ, the veil of the temple was rent in two[2].

This veil was a heavy partition curtain separating

---

[1] Exodus 34: 29,30, 35
[2] Matthew 27: 57; Mark 15: 38; Luke 23: 45

AN ACT OF COMPASSION

the holy place from the most holy, where the high priest entered once a year on the Day of Atonement with the sacrificial blood of animals to intercede on behalf of the people, so that they would receive forgiveness for their sins.

The renting of the veil signified that the sacrificial system was no longer valid. The sacrifice Christ made on our behalf eliminated the need for a human intercessor, as there was during the time of the Levitical priesthood. Jesus, being resurrected after His death, now sits at the right hand of His Father, where He assumes the role of our High Priest, making intercession for us. The Jews as a nation, however, did not accept Jesus as the Messiah. Their eyes were blinded by the veil which, symbolically, they kept over their faces, preventing them from seeing that their long-awaited Deliverer had already come.

"Notice that the text says that the veil remained 'untaken away' from their minds, even though it (the veil) was 'done away in Christ'. Here, Paul is not in any way saying that the Old Testament is done away

A REAL EYE OPENER

with. Jesus made frequent references to the Old Testament. 'Search the Scriptures', He says in John 5:39, 'for in them ye think ye have eternal life and they are they which testify of me. Again, He says In Matthew 5:17 'Think not that I am come to destroy the law or the prophets. I am not come to destroy, but to fulfil'. The Old Testament was the only scripture from which both Paul and Jesus quoted. There was no New Testament in their days. In addition, Luke 4: 16 gives clear evidence that Jesus kept the Sabbath while on earth. His disciples, after His crucifixion and ascension, also kept the Sabbath, as seen in Acts 13.

"Let me emphasize that a law *was* abolished at the cross, but it was not the Ten Commandments, as so many mistakenly believe. It was the Law of Sacrifices", the teacher explained.

"Thank you for clearing that up for me", Katherine responded.

"Let me see if I understand you correctly", George added. "God gave two separate laws?"

"Yes, He gave the Ten Commandments,

otherwise known as the Moral Law, and the Ceremonial Law, commonly referred to as Moses' Law. The Ceremonial Law is referred to as Moses' Law because Moses, at the instruction of God, wrote it in a book and used it to govern the people. It includes The Law of Sacrifices, which was made obsolete by the sacrifice of Jesus Christ to atone for our sins, but the Ten Commandments are just as valid today as when God first gave them. They will never be abolished".

"That's new information for me, thank you". George reflected.

As the class continued, Katherine seemed to be in quiet contemplation. Her expression conveyed a semblance of unease, as if irritated.

"You may be right about what you said earlier that my pastor might not be happy with my conclusion regarding the Sabbath, but I think he should know what we have discussed here today. I want to be obedient to the word of God. Pastor Kent is an excellent preacher, and a very godly man, but the information you shared with me has been a real

A REAL EYE OPENER

eye-opener. I can't believe he doesn't know all this and, I can't wait to hear what he has to say about it".

"Here is something else you might like to ponder", the teacher replied. "James 2 verse 10 says, 'Whosoever shall keep the whole law, and yet offend in one point, he is guilty of all'. In the final analysis, choosing to adhere to nine of God's commandments, as most Christians seem to do, will reap the same recompense as neglecting all 10".

"Is that right?" Katherine asked incredulously. "Does the Bible really say that if we keep all the commandments except one, we are guilty of all?"

"It sure does! As a matter fact, Katherine, why don't you find James 2: 10 and read it for us?"

Katherine was no stranger to the Bible. She found it quickly.

"That's amazing!" she exclaimed as she finished reading the text. "So then, are you telling me that if I keep all of the other nine commandments and do not keep the Sabbath, I am guilty of breaking them all, which would make me no better than a thief or a murderer?"

AN ACT OF COMPASSION

"That's putting it very bluntly, but that's not what I am telling you", the teacher replied. "That is what the word of the Lord says, as you have read. It might sound harsh, but God takes His word very seriously. God knew that, because it does not seem to hurt us, or anyone else, whether we keep the Sabbath or not, it would be the easiest of the Ten Commandments to forget. That is one of the reasons He commands us to 'remember the Sabbath day to keep it holy'. However, ignoring the Sabbath *does* hurt Someone. It hurts God.

The Sabbath is a gift to us from God. He waits for us to meet with Him on His holy day, and when we ignore it, He is disappointed. It is like rejecting a gift that your father has specially picked out and given to you. Imagine how hurt your earthly father would feel. God, our heavenly Father, also has emotions and can experience hurt, but neglecting to observe God's Sabbath not only hurts Him, it hurts us also, though we may not realize it. Celebrating the Sabbath affords us a wonderful opportunity for spiritual renewal and for physical rest and rejuvenation. It enables us to spend quality time with our Creator, who waits all week for this special day to welcome us into His rest".

"That is really something to think about", Katherine admitted.

"Yes, it is", the teacher agreed.

"But, you know, I can't deny it", she added, still baffled by the information she had just received. "I still find it very difficult to believe that God, who created human beings in His own image, and loved us enough to have given Jesus Christ His only begotten Son to die for us, could regard the keeping of a day as important as the life of a human being".

"I understand the difficulty that presents, when we look at it from a human stand-point", Elder Gibson responded. "However, when you look at the bigger picture, it is not a matter of the magnitude of the offense, as *we* see it. It is a matter of whether we choose our own way above God's. Just so you know that I am not speaking from my own opinion, let us refer to the Bible to shed some more light on just how seriously God takes His word. This might

AN ACT OF COMPASSION

surprise you--probably even shock you. I will tell you the story, but please read it for yourselves at your leisure. You will find it in the book of Numbers chapter 15, starting at verse 32.

"While the children of Israel were travelling in the wilderness, after they had received the Ten Commandments, a man went out to gather sticks on the Sabbath day. Those who saw him brought him to Moses. Moses was not sure what to do about the offence, so he put the man in ward, the text says, meaning, in detention, while he consulted with the Lord as to how to handle the matter. The word of the Lord came back to Moses saying that the man should be put to death, and he was. For breaking the Sabbath, the man received the same consequence as if he had committed murder. Very harsh, you might say, but sin in all its forms is abhorrent to God. As we discussed earlier, sin is the transgression of the law. Romans 6: 23 tells us that the wages of sin is death, but thanks be to God, the gift of God is eternal life through Jesus Christ our Lord.

"The Lord winks at the sins we commit in

A REAL EYE OPENER

ignorance, but when we know, He holds us accountable. That man knew the commandment, but defied it. Since God does not change, breaking any of His commandments is just as serious in His eyes today as it was then, although we may not reap immediate consequences". Elder Gibson explained.

"That's really serious! I never would have thought that such severe punishment could have resulted from breaking the Sabbath", Katherine admitted.

"I agree. It seems a heavy penalty, but ignoring God's word is never a light matter", the teacher responded.

"Elder Gibson", a voice spoke up with some concern, "I thought I had all my questions answered on the topic, but something else just came to my mind. Would you answer just one last one for me, please?"

"Certainly, Rebecca! Feel free to ask as many questions as you like".

"I heard a television program that spoke about the Sabbath. The preacher said that somewhere in

AN ACT OF COMPASSION

the Bible, I didn't catch exactly where, it says that no one should judge us because of a holy day, or the Sabbath day, something like that, if I'm not mistaken. Wouldn't that mean that we could choose whatever day we want to keep holy, and it would not matter?"

"Yes, yes! I think I know the text to which you are referring. I believe the preacher may have quoted Colossians 2: 16. Let us find it and see what it says. Rebecca, would you read that for us, please?"

"Sure, I'm reading from the King James Version: 'Let no man therefore judge you in meat, or in drink, or in respect of an holyday, or of the new moon, or of the sabbath days".

"Thank you. The word "sabbath" means rest. It refers not only to the weekly Sabbath on which God rested and commands us to rest, but also to other days associated with different events and ceremonies mentioned in the Bible. These were called Ceremonial Sabbaths. You will notice that the verse does not say the Sabbath *day*, but "the sabbath *days*". The Day of Atonement[1], for example, was

A REAL EYE OPENER

referred to in the Bible as a sabbath of rest.

"These sabbaths could fall on any day of the week, and sometimes only once a year, as in the case of the Day of Atonement. There were even sabbaths of rest for the land, referred to in Leviticus 26 as "your sabbaths" or 'a sabbath of rest unto the land, a Sabbath for the Lord' The sabbath of rest for the land was *one full year, and occurred only once every seven years.* The Day of Atonement, described in Leviticus 16: 29-31, occurred on the tenth day of the seventh month each year.

"On that day, the high priest made atonement for the sins of the people, by sprinkling the blood of the sin offering on the mercy seat, which covered the Ark of the Covenant, containing the Ten Commandments. The Day of Atonement, described in verse 31 as a sabbath of rest, and all the other ceremonies of the sanctuary, pointed to Jesus Christ our Great High Priest, who was offered once for the sins of the world, as Hebrews 9:28 tells us. He now sits at the right hand of our Father in heaven,

---

[1] Luke 23: 27

AN ACT OF COMPASSION

representing us before His throne, as Romans 8: 34 tells us. This is why when we pray, we address our prayers to God the Father through Jesus Christ His Son, our Mediator.

"Although the death and resurrection of Jesus Christ made the Day of Atonement unnecessary, those who had rejected Jesus as the Messiah still clung to those ordinances, perhaps imposing them on others and judging as sinners, those who did not comply. In fact, even though the earthquake that occurred at the time of Jesus' crucifixion rent the veil of the temple at Jerusalem in two, signifying the abolition of the sacrificial system, as we learn in the synoptic gospels (Matthew 27: 51, Mark 15: 38 and Luke 23: 45), animal sacrifices continued until AD 70[1], when Titus destroyed the temple at Jerusalem. Paul, who is said to have lived until AD 67 or AD 68, would no doubt have encountered those who continued to observe the Day of Atonement after

---

[1] Bible.org Article published Jan 2,000, "When did the Animal Sacrifices Stop and Why"

A REAL EYE OPENER

Jesus' resurrection.

"Another example that fits into the category of a holy day is the Passover", the teacher continued. "You no doubt have heard of it".

"Yes, I have. I know people who celebrate it", Rebecca said. "I know it's in the springtime—around April, I think, but I never asked what it meant".

"Okay, let me explain it briefly. The Passover is a feast that marked the deliverance of the Children of Israel from Egyptian bondage. At this time, God instructed the Children of Israel to kill a lamb (or a kid) for each household on the night before their departure and to put the blood upon the door post, where it could be clearly seen. On that night God sent an angel to destroy the first born of every living thing in the land of Egypt, both of man and of beast. By putting the blood on the doorpost, they would identify themselves as belonging to the children of Israel. It is called the Passover, because the destroying angel would "pass over" every house, whose doorpost was marked by the blood of the

AN ACT OF COMPASSION

lamb, sparing the lives of its inhabitants.

"The Lord commanded that this feast be celebrated on the fourteenth day of the first month each year, in remembrance of their deliverance. They were to eat the flesh of the slain animal in great haste, indicating the speed of flight by which they would escape from the land of their distress. The Passover lamb was a type of the Messiah who was to come and be slain for the sins of humanity, so that whosoever chose to accept His sacrifice would escape the penalty of sin, which is eternal death.

"The Feast of Unleavened Bread followed immediately after the Passover and lasted seven days. The Lord declared the first day of the Feast of Unleavened Bread 'a holy convocation'. On this day, the children of Israel were to do no servile work. It was a day of rest—*a* sabbath. Leviticus 23 and Exodus 12 provide all the information about the Passover. You may want to read it at your leisure.

"There are many sabbaths spoken of in the Bible, but only one that God included in the Ten Commandments, written by His own finger, to be

A REAL EYE OPENER

observed perpetually in commemoration of His creation. That Sabbath is usually referred to in the Bible as '*the* Sabbath day', '*the* Sabbath of the Lord', or '*the* Sabbath of the Lord thy God'. It is the only Sabbath instituted at creation, and was never changed or abolished, nor can it be. It will remain until the end of time and throughout eternity, because it is a reminder to the human race that God is our Creator. It is a testament to the fact that we are not the product of some giant accident of nature.

"During Paul's day, when new converts came to the Christian faith, they often encountered controversy as to what ordinances they should or should not observe. Paul, in Colossians 2: 16, was simply conveying to the people that although it was no longer necessary to observe these holy days, since their purpose had been fulfilled through Christ's atoning sacrifice, they should not allow anyone to judge them as sinners if they chose to observe certain ones of them. "Jews" who accepted Jesus Christ as the Messiah, and still kept the Passover, for example, as a part of their heritage, should not allow anyone one to judge them as any less Christian because of that choice.

"Note also, that the word we know today as "holiday" originated from the combination of the words 'holy' and 'day'. In Paul's travels, he encountered many different cultures. In this particular instance, he was addressing the Colossians, inhabitants of the city of Colossae in Turkey, Asia Minor. He wanted the followers of Christ in that region to know that celebrating their national holidays would not make them any less acceptable to Christ, as long as they refrained from practices which were contrary to the word of God.

"In addition, it is important to note that Paul was a Jew of the strictest sect-- a Pharisee. In his letter to the Philippians Chapter 3: 6, he describes himself as blameless concerning the righteousness which is of the law. The Pharisees, you may recall, were meticulous, even fanatical concerning the observance of the seventh day Sabbath. They even misguidedly opposed Jesus for healing the sick on the Sabbath day. One so highly schooled in the traditions of the Pharisees, as Paul, would never have conveyed the idea that it does not matter which day one keeps holy.

"Paul kept the Sabbath before he became a follower of Christ, and continued doing so after he became His apostle, and for the rest of his life. Acts 17:2 gives an account of Paul going into the synagogue on the Sabbath day, as his manner, (or his custom) was. That text makes it plain that he habitually went to the synagogue each Sabbath. Paul in Colossians 2: 16, was not referring to the holy Sabbath day, but to other holy days, now obsolete, and to the observance of national holidays. I hope that answers your question".

"It certainly does. Thank you very much for taking the time to answer it in such detail. I learned a lot", Rebecca replied.

"You are most welcome. Are there any other questions on this topic?" the teacher asked.

"I think that we should keep every day holy", another visitor, Jeremy, commented.

"Okay, let us see what the word of the Lord says

about that. Let us turn to Exodus 20. Jeremy, would you read verses 9 and 10, please?"

Jeremy read from the King James Version, "'Six days shalt thou labor and do all thy work, but the seventh day is the Sabbath of the Lord thy God, in it thou shalt not do any work…'"

"Thank you, Jeremy. We see here that God commands us to rest on the seventh day, but he also commands us to work on the other six days. Although, as followers of Christ, we are required to live holy lives every day, we can only keep holy that which God has made holy. God alone has the ability to confer holiness. He did not make every day holy, because He knew that it would be impossible for us to keep every day holy. We must labor in order to maintain our existence, so he gave us six ordinary days for work and one holy day for rest". Elder Gibson explained.

"I see", Jeremy nodded.

"Didn't Jesus say that the greatest commandment is to love God and to love our neighbor as ourselves?" Brad, another visitor, asked.

"I think that as long as we love God, and we are serving Him with all our hearts, and we love others, that is all we need to do".

"Thank you for that comment, Brad", Elder Gibson responded. "You are right. If we love God and are serving Him with all our hearts, that is all that matters. The question is: How do we show our love to God?"

"John 14: 15 says, 'If you love me, keep my commandments'", Sister Lafontaine responded.

Brad, who had been attending church with his wife for some time, had never been convinced that the Sabbath was still valid, and refused to relent.

"I have heard that all that God requires is that we keep one out of every seven days holy; it doesn't matter which one", Brad continued.

"That may be a very popular notion, but it is not what the Bible teaches. God blessed and set apart a particular day. The word of God says that God blessed the seventh day and made it holy. Since He made only one specific day holy, any other day of our own choosing would not be acceptable to Him",

AN ACT OF COMPASSION

Elder Gibson replied.

"I don't know exactly where it says that, but I am sure there is a text in the Bible that says that each person is free to choose whatever day they want to keep holy. Check it out. It's there somewhere", Brad continued, sticking to his position.

"You could be referring to Romans 14: 5, 6. Let's turn there and see what it says".

"One man esteemeth one day above another: another esteemeth every day alike. Let every man be fully persuaded in his own mind", Brad read from the King James Version, throwing his head back with look that clearly said, Let's see how you will answer that!

"Thank you. You have raised an excellent point. Note the words, 'Let every man be persuaded in his own mind'. Here again, Paul is referring to national or cultural festivals. He is saying that cultures where there are many such holidays, some may be considered more important than others. Therefore let everyone be persuaded in his own mind that whatever holidays he chooses to celebrate is in harmony with his conscience and with the law of God. God's Sabbath, on the other hand, is not a matter of personal choice. It is set in stone by God Himself. He commands and expects us to keep holy *the only* day that He has blessed. There can be no replacement.

At this, Brad remained silent, as if deep in thought.

Just then, Mr. Fong, another visitor commented, "It's hard to believe that the day that the Lord blessed is Saturday, not Sunday, as I had thought. Yet that is the plain truth, as the Bible teaches".

"Hi, Norman! Thank you for that comment. You have been so quiet!" Elder Gibson smiled.

"I've just been taking it all in", Norman returned.

Norman Fong, a devout follower of Christ, had always thought it a strange choice that people who profess to be servants of the Lord would congregate on Saturday instead of on the Lord's Day. Until now, there was no doubt in his mind that Sunday was the Sabbath of the Bible. Learning that there was no biblical support for Sunday observance was

AN ACT OF COMPASSION

difficult for him to accept, but there was no way of escaping the clear teaching of the Bible.

"Thank you for that observation", Elder Gibson responded. "I am happy you came here today. Now that you have knowledge of the truth, I hope that you will make the decision to follow your conviction".

"I will certainly give it serious thought", Mr. Fong replied.

"I have another question", Marissa smiled, a bit shyly.

"Okay, Marissa, let's hear it!"

"I'm not sure if this is the right time or place to ask this question, but I noticed the sign at the front, and I'm curious. What is the meaning of the name Seventh-day Adventist?"

"That is an excellent question, and an excellent time and place to ask it. I am sure you are not the only one who is curious about that. The word Adventist means one who looks forward to the second coming of Jesus Christ. Christians of many other denominations also await Christ's second coming, which means that they too, are Adventists, even though they might not call themselves by that name. We call ourselves Seventh-day Adventists, because we observe God's holy Sabbath day, which is the seventh day of the week, *and* look forward to the second coming of our Lord and Savior, Jesus Christ".

"I see. Now I understand. Thank you",

Others nodded acknowledging that they too, now understood.

"Very good", the teacher said, and then added, "Kezia, I see your hand is up, do you have a question for us?"

"No, but I have a comment", she replied.

"Okay, let's hear it", he smiled invitingly.

"Of all the great reasons for keeping God's Sabbath holy, the best is to show Him that we love Him".

"My sentiment exactly!" he responded. "If there are no further questions, we could not end on a better note".

TEN

POINTS TO PONDER

In preparing to close, Elder Gibson said, "I take it we have all had a clear understanding of what the Bible teaches regarding the importance of all God's commandments". Most of the participants nodded in agreement. "Before ending this session, however, I would like to leave you with a few other points to ponder".

"The first thing to consider is that God loves you. He loved you enough to have paid the ultimate price for your redemption. He loved you first, and desires only that you love Him in return. We show our love for God by doing what He commands, not in part, but fully.

That being said, let us remember always, that we are not saved by obeying God's law, but by accepting the atoning blood of Jesus Christ, which was shed on our behalf. We are saved by the grace of God, through faith in Jesus Christ alone. Having been saved by that precious gift of God's grace, we willingly and gladly keep His commandments. In other words, we keep His commandments, not in order to be saved, but because we have been saved.

"I am going to leave you with a few Bible references. Some we have discussed in this session and some we have not. These are just a few of the many that are interspersed throughout the Bible, regarding the permanence of God's holy day, the blessings of observing it and the consequences of not. Write them down and explore them at your leisure.

They are: Psalm 1: 1, 2; Psalm 19: 7, 8; Matthew 5: 17-19; Mk 7:7; John 14: 15; 1 John 2: 3, 4; Revelation 22:14; Psalm 119: 1; Isaiah 58: 13, 14; Hebrew 4: 9, 10 Hebrews 10: 26, 27; James 2 10-12. In addition to these texts, I will also leave you with a few points to ponder and remember.

1. The Sabbath is for humankind, not just for the Jews. God gave the Sabbath at creation before there were any Jews. The Jews descended from Abraham, long after God created the world. Mk. 2: 27 says: 'The Sabbath was made for man..."

2. The Sabbath is not a burden; it is a gift from God. God created man the day before the Sabbath, and rested with them on that first Sabbath, not because He needed to rest, but in order to spend quality time with them, and to set an example for us to follow.

3. The Sabbath is the only commandment that God emphasizes using the word 'Remember', because it is a memorial of His creation.

4. You may have heard that Jesus abolished the Ten Commandments, and replaced them with two—'love the Lord with all your heart and love your neighbor as yourself'. That is a misconception. **Jesus did not abolish any of the commandments.** He restated them in the language of love, because God is love.

5. Love to God requires that we obey all of His commandments. John 14: 15 says, 'If you love me, keep my commandments'. The first four speak of love to God; the remaining six speak of love to our fellow human beings. Love to our fellow humans requires that we respect their rights, their property, their opinions, their person, etc. If we love our neighbor, we will not kill him, steal from him, bear false witness against him, covet his goods, etc. If we love God, we will not worship other gods; neither will we hesitate to meet with Him on the day that He has set aside to commune with us in a special way. We will also honor Him by loving our fellow human beings, who, like us, are the objects of His love. Love does not invalidate any of the commandments; it encapsulates them all.

6. You may have heard it said that Jesus broke the Sabbath. That is another misconception. Mark 2:23, Matthew 12:1, and Luke 6:1 tell the story of Jesus walking through the cornfield on the Sabbath day with His disciples, who, when they became hungry, picked corn, rubbed the grains together in their hands and ate them. They did not harvest corn on the Sabbath; neither did they cook them, which would be breaking the commandment. In addition, Jesus took no part in that activity. The fanatical Pharisees' claim that He broke the Sabbath was totally unfounded. Neither He nor His disciples broke the Sabbath at that time or at any other time recorded in the Bible.

7. The Bible tells us plainly which day is the Sabbath. There are those who claim that we cannot know for sure which day is the Sabbath, because of changes in the calendar. Yet they have no difficulty recognizing Sunday as the Resurrection Day. If we are certain that Sunday is the first day of the week, the day on which Jesus rose from the dead, we should be equally certain that Saturday is the seventh, the day that God blessed and set apart as His holy day of rest.

8. Sin came into the world because of a seemingly insignificant act against the command of God. The first pair was commanded in the book of beginnings (Genesis), not to eat from the tree of the knowledge of good and evil. By disobeying that command, they lost their Eden home and their access to the tree of life. We are now admonished in the book of the end (Revelation), that in order to regain the right to the tree of life, we must obey the commandments of GOD.

9. The law cannot save us. We are saved by grace through faith, not by our own merits; it is a gift of God. However, we cannot be saved without obeying God's law. Sin cannot enter heaven, and sin is the transgression of the law. We cannot inhabit that desired country, while rebelling against the commands of its Supreme Ruler.

10. In Mark 7: 7, Jesus says, 'In vain do they worship me, teaching for doctrines

the commandments of men. You may be very surprised to discover that the doctrine of first day sacredness, as we see in most of the Christian world, is a commandment of man in direct opposition to the clear commandment of God. Speaking of which, I would like you to consider carefully the following quote. It is a statement from a newspaper article written by Priest Brady. It states:

'It is well to remind the Presbyterians, Baptists, Methodists, and all other Christians, that the Bible does not support them anywhere in their observance of Sunday. Sunday is an institution of the Roman Catholic Church and those who observe the day observe a commandment of the Catholic Church[1] '".

At this, a gasp emitted from the class.

The teacher continued: "Here is another statement you might like to ponder. It is a quote from a lecture given in 1893 by Bishop T. Enright. It states:

'I have repeatedly offered $1,000 to anyone who can prove to me from the Bible

---

Priest Brady in an address reported in The News, Elizabeth, New Jersey: 1903 *alone that I am bound to keep Sunday holy. There is no such law in the Bible. It is a law of the holy Catholic Church alone. The Bible says, 'Remember the Sabbath day to keep it holy.' The Catholic Church says: 'No. By my divine power I abolish the Sabbath day and command you to keep holy the first day of the week.' And lo! The entire civilized world bows down in a reverent obedience to the command of the holy Catholic Church[1]"'.*

"That's astonishing!" Katherine exclaimed in utter disbelief.

"If you were shocked by the former statements, here is yet another article by Bishop T. Enright you might also want to consider", the teacher added:

'There is but one church on the face of the earth which has the power, or claims power, to make laws binding on the conscience, binding before God, binding under penalty of hell-fire; for instance, the institution of Sunday. What right has any other church to keep this day? You answer by virtue of the third commandment [the Papacy renamed the fourth commandment, calling it the third], which says, 'Remember that thou

---

[1] Bishop T, Enright C.S.s.R in a lecture at Hartford, Kansas, February 18, 1884

keep holy the Sabbath day.' But Sunday is not the Sabbath. Any schoolboy knows that Sunday is the first day of the week. I have repeatedly offered one thousand dollars to anyone who will prove by the Bible alone that Sunday is the day we are bound to keep, and no one has called for the money. It was the holy Catholic Church that changed the day of rest from Saturday, the seventh day, to Sunday, the first day of the week[1]'.

The teacher also pointed out the following two statements by another representative of that organization which further surprised everyone.

'You may read the Bible from Genesis to Revelation, and you will not find a single line authorizing the sanctification of Sunday. The Scriptures enforce the religious observance of Saturday, a day which we never sanctify[2]'.

'The Catholic Church for over one thousand years before the existence of a

---

Bishop T. Enright, C.S.s.R. in a Lecture delivered in 1893

[2] The Faith of Our Fathers, by James Cardinal Gibbons, Archbishop of Baltimore, 88th edition, page 89. Originally published in 1876, republished and Copyright 1980 by TAN Books and Publishers, Inc., pages 72-73.

AN ACT OF COMPASSION

> *Protestant, by virtue of her divine mission, changed the day from Saturday to Sunday*[1].

"As you can see", Elder Gibson continued, "this organization is very frank in admitting its role in conveying to the world the misconception that God's Sabbath has been changed from Saturday to Sunday. The Sabbath remains the seventh day, despite man's attempt to change it. What God has put in place, no person or group of persons has the authority to replace. God's seventh-day Sabbath is as valid today as it ever was.

Another crucial fact of which most Christians might not be aware is that the Sabbath question will play a very significant role in end time events. The time is fast approaching when each individual must make a definite choice. We each must choose where our loyalty will fall—on the side of God, or on that of man. I hope we will say like Peter and the apostles in Acts 5: 29, 'we ought to obey God rather than men'.

---

[1] The Catholic Mirror, September 23, 1893

POINTS TO PONDER

"There is no better time than the present to make the choice to obey God, while the winds of strife that are soon to be unleashed upon the world are held in check. If we do not, like Daniel, purpose now in our hearts to stand for that which is right in the sight of God, we will not be able to stand the test when it comes.

There is so much more that could be said on this subject, but for now, I think we have covered sufficient information for anyone to process. We may have to continue this discussion in another session.

If we take away nothing else from this study today, let us never forget that although the law cannot save us, for we are saved *only* by the grace of God, through faith in Jesus Christ, **we cannot inhabit the heavenly kingdom without keeping the law**. We are saved by grace, but we are rewarded according to our works.

Let us reflect on these points, and I pray that everyone present will make the decision, difficult as it may be, to take a stand on the side of truth—to

AN ACT OF COMPASSION

take a stand for God. If after having knowledge of the truth, we neglect to follow it, we are without excuse, as Hebrews 10: 26 indicates.

"We have now come to the end of our Bible study. Thank you for your participation. Join us again next week for another exciting session. Visitors, it was a great pleasure having you. Although Vacation Bible School has ended, I hope we will not have seen the last of you. Feel free to visit anytime. May GOD guide you as you seek to do His will. Let us pray".

"Father in heaven, I thank You for the privilege of studying Your holy word, and for all who participated in this study. Help us to do Your commandments, so that we may have right to the tree of life and may enter in through the gates into that bright city, the new Jerusalem, when Jesus returns to claim His faithful followers. We ask this in His redeeming name. Amen".

ELEVEN
OLD THINGS ARE PAST AWAY

The group dispersed silently. Everyone appeared to be in deep thought, trying to digest the new information, especially regarding the quotations Elder Gibson read. The following week, the McBride family began Bible study in their home, meeting once a week with John, the teacher assigned to them. The pastor also continued to visit from time to time, offering spiritual guidance.

As they learned more about the Sabbath, it felt strange even thinking of everyday activities on Saturdays. They had come to the full acceptance of Jesus Christ as their Savior, and of the Sabbath as God's holy day of rest. They now knew that, except in cases of emergency no work should be done on that day.

AN ACT OF COMPASSION

Matthew gradually gave up going to the pub to drink with his friends. He still went occasionally to see them, but instead of his regular drink, he would order a root beer. In addition to that, his conversation now centered upon the love of Jesus Christ.

With his interest in going to the pub now greatly reduced, he spent most of his spare time reading the Bible and other inspirational literature. He had also learned how to pray, and pray he did. He prayed for forgiveness, for deliverance, for guidance and for the revelation of God's will for his life.

God revealed to him His great love and power, by granting his request for deliverance. He became completely sober without the help of any counseling. The bottle, which he once loved and hated, he now totally abhorred.

Early one morning, as Rebecca went to the kitchen to prepare breakfast before heading off to work, to her surprise, she saw her husband standing at the sink pouring down the drain every bottle of his prized collection of wine that he had aged and kept

OLD THINGS ARE PAST AWAY

for years. She could hardly believe her eyes.

"Matthew, you're throwing out all your wine!" She exclaimed.

"Why not?" He smiled. "If any man be in Christ, he is a new creature. Old things are passed away. Why hold on to the past?"

"I totally agree", Rebecca smiled back.

She rejoiced at the change that had come over her husband, and that they had once again found a common interest and were walking the same path. She knew that God had worked a miracle in their lives, which greatly increased her faith in Him.

Matthew, on his part, gave thanks to God for the new man that he had become. The knowledge of the word of God gave him a freedom and a confidence he had never known before. He was excited and amazed to discover the treasures contained in the Bible, he told the teacher.

After some time of Bible study, being fully convinced of the truth of God's word and of His great love for them, and having accepted Jesus Christ as their personal Savior, the family requested

AN ACT OF COMPASSION

baptism. They looked forward, with great anticipation, to the day when, together they would make a public declaration of their decision to follow Jesus all the way. The teacher was thrilled.

Not everyone shared Matthew's joy, however. When he told his friends about his upcoming baptism, the mixed reaction he received did not surprise him. His teacher, John had prepared him for the challenges he would face.

He had alerted him to the wiles that the devil, the enemy of man, would use in trying to discourage him from serving God. He had given him the assurance that he needed not fear, because Jesus would be with him always to strengthen him. He had told Matthew that nothing would be able to separate him from the fold of God, as long as he continued to put his trust in Him.

Because of the preparation he received, when his best friend Shane withdrew his friendship, it hurt, but he understood. The realization that they would no longer be able to drink together had hit Shane hard. Matthew had decided to be baptized. This was serious, Shane realized. There would be no turning back now. He was not going through a phase, as Shane had first thought. It was for real. Eventually, he stopped calling, and would no longer receive or return Matthew's calls. "A buddy is no buddy, if he can't share a beer", he had told Matthew the last time they spoke.

Matthew took no offence. He prayed for the revelation of God's truth to his friend, whom he loved dearly, but whose company he would no longer be able to share, at least for the present time. He hoped it would only be temporary, and decided to give him space, as he continued to pray for him.

Jason saw it differently. The trio had been hanging out together since their college days, and he treasured his friendship with both Shane and Matthew. It made him sad to see their relationship end.

"You know, Matt", he said, when he heard the news of Matthew's decision to be baptized, "this might seem strange to you, but I think it's wonderful that you're going to be baptized. It's too bad that

Shane finds it so hard to accept".

"Do you really mean that? You're happy I'm getting baptized?" Matthew asked, surprised.

"Well, yeah! I believe there is a God, and I think it's good that you have decided to follow Him".

"Really? I'm so happy to hear that! It's good to know that you believe in God".

"When I was little I learned about God in Sunday School".

"Yeah? What did you learn?"

"I learned that Jesus died for the sins of the world and that He rose again and went to heaven. I heard that He is coming back to earth again. I had heard that He was supposed to come back in 2012. I don't know why He didn't come, but I still believe in Him".

"Did you grow up in a Christian home?" Matthew asked, deliberately overlooking the statement concerning the time of Christ's return. He hoped that there would be another opportunity to let him know that no one knows that time.

"No, I didn't, but I went to Sunday school a few

OLD THINGS ARE PAST AWAY

times with my neighbor Kirk and his parents when I was about five, or so".

"I see. Would you like to learn more about Jesus?"

"You know, it's funny you should ask".

"Why's that?"

"Well, would you believe it? I have always wondered how to become a Christian, but no one ever told me. I know that there are people who knock on doors and tell people about Jesus, but no one ever came to my door; at least, not that I know of. They could have come when I was out and I missed them". Jason said with a hint of sadness in his voice.

"Would you like to have someone study the Bible with you? I had a great teacher! Maybe I could link you up with him", Matthew offered.

"That would be super!" Jason said excitedly.

"Great! Would you like to come with me to church some time? That way you could meet the pastor, or the elder I studied with, likely both. They would be happy to arrange Bible study for you. If you would rather not come to church, I could let them know you're interested, and someone would contact you and arrange to study with you at home".

"I wouldn't mind going to church with you. Would it have to be on a Saturday, though? I know you go to church on Saturdays".

"Not necessarily. We meet during the week also. By the way, would you like to come to my baptism?"

"I'd love to! Thank you! Even though my parents were not church-goers in the true sense, they had me baptized when I was a baby, but I have never seen a baptism. I think it would be an awesome experience for me", Jason replied eagerly.

"Wonderful! I'll let you know the date". Matthew, like Jason, had never witnessed a baptism. He was excited that not only was he going to witness one, he was also going to experience it at the same time. Again, he did not let Jason know that infant baptism was not biblical. He knew that by studying the Bible, he would soon come to that knowledge.

Jason made plans to go with Matthew to the

OLD THINGS ARE PAST AWAY

Wednesday evening meeting the following week. Accompanied by Marissa, Matthew picked him up after work. Rebecca could not join them, since she had to work.

As Jason entered the building, he felt a sense of satisfaction, knowing he was on his way to doing something positively life-changing. Being always thrilled to have new visitors, the group lavished attention upon him. The pastor greeted him warmly, encouraged him, and introduced him to his Bible worker, Paul Jacobs, who arranged to meet with him at the time and place of his choice.

Jason chose to do his Bible study at a location away from home. Faced with the possibility that his wife might react unfavorably, he wanted to avoid her knowing. In fact, he was not ready to make his interest known to anyone just yet. For now, it would be between him and Matthew--and the Bible worker, of course.

He arranged to meet with Paul at a nearby diner after work, on Tuesday evenings at 5:30 p.m. This would work perfectly for him. Since he frequently

AN ACT OF COMPASSION

worked overtime, he would just replace some of those hours with his Bible study. In so doing, there would be no change in the time he would normally arrive at home, and therefore, no need for an explanation.

As they arrived at the diner, the Bible worker felt a bit ill at ease. He had been used to conducting Bible studies either at the church, in people's homes or, on rare occasions, in his own home, but he reminded himself of instances in the Bible where Jesus ministered to people in unlikely places. He called to mind Jesus eating at the house of Zacchaeus the publican, attending a feast at the house of Simon, the leper, and eating with publicans.

He knew that it was acceptable to reach people on their own grounds, as long as he did not participate in any activity of theirs that would compromise his convictions. The test came sooner than he had anticipated.

"Have a seat, please", Jason motioned to him, placing himself in his old familiar corner, close to the bar.

"Thank you", Paul smiled, as he sat.

"Mr. Jacobs, ---"Jason began.

"Paul, please", Paul interrupted.

"Okay. Paul, may I offer you a cup of coffee before we begin, or would you prefer something from the bar? I am going to have some coffee myself. They have great flavors here. Hazelnut is my favorite. Do you have a favorite?"

"Thank you, that's very kind of you, but I abstain from caffeine and alcohol altogether".

"You mean you don't drink *any* coffee at all?" Jason asked.

"Yes, that's right. I abstain from all caffeinated beverages", Paul replied, as he fished out his pen and note pad from his brief case.

"Really? I don't think I could *ever* do that. How do you get through the day?" Jason asked.

"Quite easily, as a matter of fact", Paul smiled. "We'll talk about that some other time. I could use a glass of water, though, if you don't mind".

"Not at all! Hey, Ronny!" Jason called, as the

AN ACT OF COMPASSION

waiter finished taking an order and was about to return to the kitchen.

"Jason! How's it going, pal?" Ronny smiled cheerily, as he came toward Jason's table.

"It's going well. How is it going with you?" Jason returned.

"Can't complain. How may I serve you today?" Ronny asked in his most professional tone, noticing Jason's guest.

"The usual for me, and a bottle of spring water for the gentleman, please", Jason returned, being careful not to introduce his guest.

"Okay. Be back in a mome", Ronny smiled curiously, making his way to the kitchen.

In the meantime, Jason wondered if he might have made a mistake meeting at the diner, after all. Too many people knew him there. He did not particularly want them to know he was doing Bible study. He thought of the library, but it was always crowded at that time of day, so that would not work. Well, maybe the guys would just think he was buying life insurance, or something, he hoped.

OLD THINGS ARE PAST AWAY

As Paul opened his brief case and retrieved his Bible and the first lesson, Ronny returned with their order. Setting down the coffee in front of Jason and the water in front of Paul, he gave a curious frown, which quickly turned into a smile, as they both looked up at him to say thanks. Jason caught that.

"Ron's my old buddy; he'll probably give me a good ribbing, having seen the Bible, but I'm prepared", Jason said, putting on a brave smile, as Ron left the table.

"It feels kind of strange for me being here also, I must admit", Paul said. "I'm almost thinking we could go to my place, but my two year old would win the competition for my attention, guaranteed".

"That won't be necessary. I think we'll do just fine here", Jason said, taking a sip of his coffee, as he scanned the place with his eyes. "Everyone here is quite nice, actually".

"Before we begin, I would like to seek the Lord's guidance in prayer. Will you join me?" Paul invited.

"Sure", Jason gulped, setting down his cup and

masking his uneasiness with an appearance of calm that could win him an academy award for best actor.

Before praying, Paul read Psalm 19 from the King James Version of the Holy Bible. "The heavens declare the glory of God and the firmament showeth His handiwork...." Following the prayer, he opened the study guide and read the introduction.

As he read, he noticed that a couple sitting close by, kept their eyes on him, as if paying close attention to what he was saying. As they proceeded through the lesson, the man got up and stood by their table, unabashedly reading over Paul's shoulder. Startled, Jason shot him a quizzical frown.

"May we help you?" he demanded, making no effort to disguise his displeasure.

"I'm sorry. I couldn't help noticing the title on the cover of the book your friend is reading from. Forgive me. I totally forgot my manners", the man replied sheepishly.

"We're doing a Bible study here", Jason informed him, casting aside his initial feeling of awkwardness. He was sure that that would send the intruder packing.

"A Bible study? Fascinating!" the man exclaimed.

"You're interested in the Bible too?"Jason asked, taken aback.

"Oh, yes! I'm curious. I've always been puzzled by the origin of life, and I heard somewhere that the Bible has the answer. I've never read the Bible, so I don't know, but I sure would like to find out. The booklet your friend was reading from caught my eye, because of the title: 'Where Did We Come From?' That's the million-dollar question for me. I'd love to know the answer".

He was not one of the regulars, but he seemed like a very nice man, so Jason decided to overlook his audacity, but was not sure how Paul felt about it.

TWELVE
THE LITTLE GROUP

Jason and Paul looked at each other.

"Would you like to join us?" Jason invited.

"You don't mind?" the stranger asked.

"Well, I really wanted all of my teacher's attention, I must admit, but I can't be selfish studying the word of God, can I?" Jason smiled. "So Paul, if that's okay with you…"

"Sure", Paul interjected, "if it's okay with you, it's fine with me".

"Can my wife join, too?" the man asked eagerly.

"Certainly!" Paul and Jason chorused.

"Thank you". Smiling, the man hurried back to his table and quickly returned with his wife.

"I'm Jason, and this is my Bible instructor, Paul", Jason introduced, as the man and his wife approached.

"I'm Todd and this is my wife Kelley", the man returned. "Sorry for the intrusion", he apologized, as they exchanged handshakes. "I don't do that very often. I am really a nice guy. Thank you for being so kind. For a moment there, I thought you might have decked me one—not that I wouldn't have deserved it", he joked, his eyes on Jason.

"I'm a lover, not a fighter", Jason laughed, joined by the others.

"Not to worry", Paul reassured him. "Welcome to our table".

"Thank you so much. I've often wondered if there really was a God, but I have also questioned the soundness of the Theory of Evolution. When I overheard you reading that a Master Designer created the world, I could not resist. I had to hear the rest, which I could not hear clearly from my table, hence my reason for intruding. That's a fascinating topic".

"Indeed it is", the teacher agreed. "The question of how life originated is one that I believe has

AN ACT OF COMPASSION

always puzzled even the most brilliant scientific minds. Even those who accept the Darwinian explanation know that there are missing parts of the puzzle. We believe in the biblical account".

"I find that very intriguing", Todd responded.

Todd, who had always prided himself in the fact that somewhere in his genealogy he had a connection to royalty, could not bring himself to accept the idea that his umpteen billionth great grandpapa to the power of 10 was none other than His Royal Majesty, King Tadpole of Slime Land. That just did not sit well with him. He did not like frogs, and certainly did not want to be related to them.

It gave him great comfort to think that he owed his existence to an intelligent, all powerful Master Designer who loves and cares for the works of His hands. He would much rather be the product of the well-ordered plan of such a Being, than an accident of some colossal explosion known as the Big Bang. His primary concern had always been, "Where did these colliding substances come from that caused this explosion?" No one could provide him with a convincing answer, so he, like many of his colleagues, remained baffled as to the origin of life. He was excited to think that his search for truth might end at this little corner diner.

At the end of the lesson, he asked to join them for the next session, to which they readily consented. So Todd and his wife returned the following Tuesday, and continued attending until the end of the course.

As time went on, other patrons at the diner noticed the intensity of the discussions, and became curious. They noticed also that Jason, a regular at the diner, adopted a new way of speaking. He hardly swore at all any more, even when Paul was not around--not even when he made what he called his killer shots at the pool table. Some of the men he regularly sat with were the first to notice, but to his surprise, the owner of the diner, Sadat also noticed.

"What has happened to you, man?" Sadat asked jokingly during a game of pool.

"What do you mean?" Jason replied, not being

conscious of the change in his own behavior.

"Well, to put it bluntly, you have not assaulted my ears once during this entire game, much to my relief, I must admit", Sadat chuckled.

"Yeah, that's right! Come to think of it, I haven't!"

"How come? Not that I'm complaining!"

"Well, it's like this: I met someone", Jason replied, a bit timidly.

"You met someone? What do you mean you met someone? Are you nuts? You're not…?" Sadat looked at Jason under his eyes.

"No! I could never ask for a better wife", Jason quickly interrupted. "That's not it at all!"

"It isn't? You just told me you met someone, and that is why you are acting so pleasantly strange. So if that's not it, what *is* it?"

The two had been playing pool together for a while, and had developed somewhat of a relationship between them. Sadat knew Jason to be a good pool player, who never concealed his excitement whenever he made a great shot or won a

THE LITTLE GROUP

game. He found it strange hearing him simply exclaim, "Yessss!" or "Aright!" when he made a shot, instead of his usual favorite expletive. Hearing him say that he met someone, Sadat found even stranger. He had always thought of Jason as a decent fellow, apart from his sometimes crass vocabulary. He liked Jason. He would never associate him with infidelity, and would certainly not condone it.

"Yeah, I did say that I met Someone", Jason affirmed.

"Oh no, don't tell me you're…" Sadat began.

"Oh, no, no! You're way off, man!" Jason again interrupted. "I've heard it said that people who are that way were born that way. Some say that it's a choice. I don't know the answer to that, but whatever the reason, that just does not seem right to me", Jason commented, though not yet familiar with Leviticus 18:22, which provides the answer.

"Thank God!" Sadat muttered under his breath. "Well, then, what do you mean, you met someone?"

"Do you really want to know?" Jason asked, not having the confidence to tell Sadat plainly that he had met Jesus Christ, and that the change in him was due to the working of the Holy Spirit in his life.

"Now you're going to make *me* swear! Out with it, man! What do you mean do I really want to know? Of course, I want to know! This suspense is driving me crazy".

"Are you going to be at the diner next Tuesday evening?"

"I was not planning on it. Why?"

"If you are here next Tuesday, you'll find out".

"That's all you're going to tell me?"

"'Yes, that's it for now".

"Now I'm *really* curious! Listen buddy, my favorite game is pool. You know that. I like golf too, but I'm definitely *not* enjoying this game you're playing. I'll be here next Tuesday, and whatever the answer to this big puzzle is, it had better be good!" Sadat cautioned, half-jokingly.

"I wish I could tell you more, but it's not a good time right now", Jason said apologetically.

"Okay, I guess I'll have to wait then", Sadat replied, trying to figure out what he might be about to discover.

"By the way, did I hear you say, 'Thank God', a moment ago?" Jason asked.

"When? Oh, you mean when I found out I was wrong about what I thought you were trying to tell me? Yeah, I said that! Why?"

"You believe in God, then?"

"Oh, that's just an expression. I really do not know what I believe where religion is concerned. I was just relieved to know that you were not involved in what came to my mind. You know what I mean".

"Yeah, I know what you mean. Well, see you next Tuesday, Old Chum", Jason said with a grin, trying hard to imitate a British accent and failing miserably.

Amused, Sadat waved good-bye as he walked to his car.

"What have I done?" the thought hit Jason right after Sadat left. "I'm inviting Sadat to a Bible study session held in his own diner, without him knowing! That was not very smart. I think I might have just got both myself and Paul in a pickle. People meet here all the time for business transactions, but this is different. I don't know if Sadat would object, but I think I'd better be straight with him". Jason ran out to the parking lot, frantically trying to catch up to Sadat, but it was too late. Sadat was gone. He had reached the parking lot just in time to see him completing his right turn on to the street.

"Okay, then", Jason thought. "I'd better let Paul know what I did, so he would not be surprised, in case Sadat throws us out on our ears next Tuesday, as he well might".

Reaching for his cell phone, he dialed Paul's number. In the middle of dinner, Paul's wife picked up the phone.

"Hello, may I speak to Mr. Abrahams, please?"Jason asked shyly.

"I'm afraid he is not available at the moment. Could he call you back?"

Paul had never liked interruptions during a meal.

"Sure", Jason answered, disappointed at not being able to speak to Paul immediately.

"Your name and telephone number, please?"

THE LITTLE GROUP

"My name is Jason Timberbank, and my number is …"

"Okay, let me just write that down. Jason Timber…" she repeated as she wrote.

"Jason?" Paul interrupted, his mouth half full.

"Yes, Jason Timberbank", his wife repeated. "Do you know him?"

Motioning to her to hand him the phone, he reached out and took it while he swallowed. "He's one of my Bible students".

"Hi, Jason. How's it going?" Paul asked a bit puzzled. Jason had never called him at home before.

"Hi Paul, I'm sorry to bother you".

"It's no bother. Is everything okay?"

"I think I made a bit of a booboo that you ought to know about".

"What happened?"

"To make a long story short, I invited the owner of the diner to meet with me there next week, but I did not tell him I was inviting him to our Bible study group".

"How did you manage that?"

AN ACT OF COMPASSION

"Well, we play pool together, and he noticed that I don't use the same expressions as before. He commented on the difference and wanted to know what caused it. For some reason, I did not have the courage to tell him directly, so I told him I met Someone, and invited him to come and see. I didn't want to tell him about our group, in case he objected to our meeting there. Afterwards it occurred to me that I might have made a huge mistake, which could bring about the very thing I was trying to avoid. I should have been up front with him, I'm sorry".

Although Paul understood Jason's reasoning, and the initial shyness that a new believer often experiences, he would have preferred him to have been forthright with Sadat, but trusted in the Lord that all would be well. Jason, on the other hand, worried that he may have ruined a good thing. He wished he had been more courageous.

"Don't worry about it, Jason", Paul reassured him. "If it should happen that we can't meet there any more, we'll work something out. The Lord will see us through".

"Thanks for understanding, Paul".

"No problem. We'll see you on Tuesday, then. Take care. God's peace be with you".

Thank you", Jason replied, with a sigh of relief at Paul's comforting words.

"You are really bold, you know that?" Sadat said to Jason, as the class concluded the following Tuesday.

"Yeah, I know", Jason admitted, his head down. "After you left on Wednesday, I thought I had made a mistake in not being straight with you. I tried to catch up with you to tell you, but I missed you by a split second".

"It was probably good that you did. When you invited me to this table, I complied out of curiosity. I was really anxious to find out who that mystery person was that you had met. When I found out what it was all about, I was not too happy, but I decided to stay for a little while, just to be polite, and deal with you later. I wasn't sure how I would get back at you, but I sure was thinking about it. I must admit, though, I found the discussion very interesting, as you can probably tell by the fact that I am still sitting here, and so are *you*, if you catch my drift", Sadat chuckled.

"So we are safe, then?" Jason asked sheepishly.

"You're safe", Sadat winked.

"Thanks, man", Jason smiled.

"You are most welcome", Sadat returned.

"I hope you'll be able to join us again next week, Sadat. It was a real pleasure having you with us today. If you enjoyed this session, you will enjoy the next one even more. It gets better every time", the teacher invited.

"I can't say that I'll be back. The discussion was interesting, but I'm not a Christian".

"That's alright. We value your company regardless of religion", Paul replied.

"Thank you. I was brought up with a different system of beliefs, but I like to learn, and I'm always interested in what other people believe. If I am here, next time, I wouldn't mind hearing what else you have to say, but I won't make you any promises".

"That's okay. If you choose to sit in on our

THE LITTLE GROUP

discussion, we would be happy to have you anytime". Paul smiled.

"Thank you". Sadat replied.

"Thank you for allowing us to use your establishment", Paul added.

"Not a problem. As a matter of fact, the pleasure is mine. You are increasing my business!"

"That's wonderful!" Paul smiled.

"Now I must take my leave of your lovely company. I'm going to pop by the kitchen and say hi to Chef. Have a good evening". Sadat bowed politely.

"Hope to see you soon for another game of pool", Jason called as Sadat walked toward the kitchen.

"Sure thing, mate!" Sadat called back.

To Jason's surprise, Sadat returned the following week, and to everyone's greater surprise, ended up joining the group! Over the course of the following weeks, Sadat found himself asking many questions about things that had always baffled him, and receiving convincing answers. Contrary to his

AN ACT OF COMPASSION

former beliefs that Jesus was just a good man and a prophet and that the Bible could not be trusted because it had been changed many times, he came to realize the following important truths:

1. If Jesus was not the Son of God as He said, He would have been a great deceiver, who tricked the entire world. This would not be characteristic of a good man. If not a deceiver, He would have been a mad man, claiming to be someone He was not. No one considers liars or lunatics to be admirable or trustworthy.

2. No change in any part of the Bible has affected its main theme—God's love for humankind, the promise of a Savior, the sacrifice of Jesus Christ to atone for the sins of humanity, His offer of the free gift of salvation to all who will accept it, and His promise to return to earth to receive those who have accepted His offer of eternal life.

Since he believed that Jesus was indeed a good man, and neither a liar nor a lunatic, he concluded that He must have been the Son of God, as He said[1]. He had now become open to the idea that Jesus Christ might be the One through Whom alone salvation comes, but he still had questions. His curiosity being aroused, he was not content to stop at the information he had gained from the Bible study group. Hungrier for knowledge than he had ever been, he studied the Bible ardently.

By the end of the course, the group had expanded to 14, including one of the waiters. It became necessary to change the venue from the diner to the church and from Tuesdays to Sunday evenings. Jason's wife, now being aware of his interest, also joined the group, but mainly to accompany her husband. She made it clear from the beginning that she had no interest in studying the Bible. She could not let go of the ingrained idea that, since she was living an honest life and was not doing

---

[1] John 10: 36

harm to anyone, she had no need to change. She would argue that if God is fair, he will judge her based on the life that she has lived, and will reward her accordingly. That was a step up from her original belief that she was her own god, which she supported by quoting Psalm 82: 6.

Jason, having now fully accepted the truth of salvation through Jesus Christ, spent much time in prayer for his wife. It would be his greatest delight if she would also come to accept this wonderful gift. If God saw it fit to bless them with children, he would like them to have God-fearing parents. Paul, being aware of Jason's concern, brought the matter to his prayer group, who prayed fervently that she would heed the call of the Holy Spirit and surrender her life to Christ.

Jason was happy when she agreed to accompany him to Matthew's baptism. "At least she would hear a sermon, and who knows?" he thought. He had heard that God moves in mysterious ways to accomplish His purpose. At the baptism, hearing Matthew take his vows and seeing him submerged in

THE LITTLE GROUP

the water, deeply moved them both. At the same time, it made her very uncomfortable. She realized that soon she would be witnessing her husband do the same. Fear took hold of her. What will life be like then? That would be the end of their fun times together. Jason reassured her that the good times would not end; they would be different, but better.

A few weeks after the baptism of Matthew and his family, the Diner Bible Class as it came to be known, ended with very encouraging results. That study group saw five people baptized, including one of the waiters at the diner, named Larry. And, to the surprise of everyone—including himself, Sadat!

God had blessed Jason's simple expression of a desire to know more about Him, with an abundant harvest. This occurred only because Matthew Mc Bride, having made public his decision to follow Jesus, had sparked the interest of his friend, Jason, who had a thirst for the Living Water, and needed only to have the way to the Fountain of Life opened up to him. The opportunity came, and he took it, leading many others to share in its never-ending flow.

As Jason continued to pray for his wife, God heard his prayer beyond his expectation. Despite her reluctance to yield her life to any power outside of herself, Jolene continued to accompany her husband to the Bible study group. On the day of his baptism, the pastor made an appeal inviting everyone who would like to take a stand for Jesus to come forward.

Jolene seemed restless, uneasy. She had been hearing the call of the Holy Spirit during the Bible study, but had been resisting. She did not know if she could commit to living the life required of a follower of Christ, not only because of the pleasures she thought she would have to give up, but because she found it difficult to yield control to a higher power. As the appeal continued, her conviction grew stronger.

Palms now sweating, thumbs twiddling she could stand it no longer. She wanted to run out of the building. She got up, started toward the front door, then suddenly turned and made her way to the poolside. It was as if the Holy Spirit had guided her

THE LITTLE GROUP

there. Hands trembling, tears streaming down her face, she surrendered her life to Christ, to the great surprise of everyone, and the inexpressible joy of her husband. In that moment, his faith greatly increased. He now had living proof of the power of prayer. God had just answered his.

Although not everyone who attended the group took the vow to follow Jesus all the way, all, especially Todd and Kelley, felt a true sense of accomplishment. They had received answers to many puzzling questions. They treasured the knowledge they had gained, and decided to continue reading the Bible. They were convinced of the truth, but were reluctant to associate themselves with any church group just yet, they told Paul.

At the end of the course, everyone received a certificate. Unfortunately, some of those who hesitated to take the step of baptism mistakenly believed that they had obstacles in their paths that would hinder them from coming to Jesus. These did not comprehend His ability and desire to cleanse from all unrighteousness every life surrendered to

AN ACT OF COMPASSION

His control. Others, despite having a real sense that God loved them and wanted them to be saved in His kingdom, were not ready to let go of their present lifestyles. They had not yet come to the recognition of the fullness of joy they would experience in the presence of God, and the endless pleasures they would find at His right hand. The church prayed that they would make their decision for Christ, while the word of God was still fresh in their minds, and while the opportunity was still available.

The week following their baptism, the Mc Bride family had received their official welcome into the membership of the church. At this time they had attended a fellowship luncheon, which took place after the service. All the members had come together for a family reunion, the Mc Brides being the center of attention.

Jason, having been present on that occasion, had described it as an experience he would never forget. He had only just begun his Bible study at that time, but knew that one day he too, would receive the right hand of fellowship into the family of God, and had looked forward to his own official welcome with eager anticipation.

He had no idea how special *his* day was going to be. A week after his baptism, he, along with his wife and all the newly baptized in his group, received a joyous welcome into the church family. All the participants in his group attended church that day, including those who did chose not to be baptized.

Adding Jason and his group to their membership greatly delighted the congregation. With his wife, Jolene by his side, Jason's joy at that moment could only have been surpassed by that of Jesus and the angels in heaven, as He welcomed His lost sheep home.

As for the Mc Bride family, on the day of their baptism David and Leah La Fontaine had celebrated their twentieth wedding anniversary. The Lafontaines had invited the congregation to their home for the celebration, which took place at the end of the Sabbath. At that gathering, everyone had a great time getting better acquainted with each other in a social setting. Matthew surprised them all

AN ACT OF COMPASSION

with his talent for singing and playing the guitar. His melodious tenor voice rang through the house and generated showers of applause. Not surprisingly, Candace, the choir director recruited him immediately, much to his delight. Dale, the music coordinator, also assigned him to sing during one of the upcoming events.

He had not sung in public before, except for Karaoke Hour at his former favorite bar, but despite his apprehension, he willingly accepted. In times past, he had enjoyed singing and playing Rock, Country/Western and Rhythm and Blues on his guitar. Playing the guitar was one of his favorite hobbies. He now sang songs of praise to God, still playing his guitar, but with a different tune.

Before drinking took over Matthew's life, Marissa and her mother had enjoyed his singing and playing. They had missed the evenings when they would sit around in the den, and he would entertain them. Now it gave them far greater pleasure to listen to him. The words of the songs he now sang, as well as the music, not only gave them great pleasure, but

THE LITTLE GROUP

also ushered in an atmosphere of peace and tranquility to their household, that they had not experienced in times past. It sometimes brought tears of joy to Rebecca, knowing how far they had all come.

Matthew's life now led him in a new direction. He no longer needed the bottle. He had found a new Friend--a true Friend in Jesus Christ. He had prayed for deliverance and had received it. He no longer had any reason to be ashamed or to think little of himself. He felt secure that Jesus loved him and had a plan for his life.

Although many of the people with whom he associated during his drinking days did not understand or accept his new lifestyle, he kept in touch with all who would allow him, and shared his newfound faith with those who would listen. He longed for them to experience the joy of salvation that he had come to know.

Having played even a small part in Jason's and his wife's acceptance of Jesus Christ as their personal Savior, gave Matthew unspeakable joy. He wanted to see yet others rescued from the valley of despair from which he had been lifted.

Along with Jason, two of Matthew's former drinking buddies had attended his baptism. One of them took his baptismal vows at the time that Jason did. That also brought great joy to Matthew's heart, but his interest in sharing his new experience went even beyond witnessing.

After his baptism, a great zeal to liberate those still trapped in the prison of alcoholism took hold of him. He started volunteering several hours a week helping the homeless, especially those who had become that way because of some kind of substance abuse, especially alcohol. With the help of his wife, his daughter and the Lafontaines, along with assistance from other church members, he eventually established a facility for the distribution of food and clothing to the needy.

Most of the recipients of this service were homeless alcoholics with whom he identified. He was an alcoholic, who, though not presently trapped in that vice, was still on the verge of losing his home

THE LITTLE GROUP

because of alcohol. While searching for gainful employment, he enlisted the aid of anyone who would lend a helping hand in the project of his passion. Whosoever was willing, there was work for them to do.

This project saw the transformation of many lives, both from the volunteers and from those whom they served. In addition to meeting the physical needs of people whose lives were broken by dire circumstances, this organization also aimed at addressing their psychological, emotional, social and spiritual needs.

Matthew had come to appreciate greatly the power of prayer. He had never forgotten his first experience of hearing someone pray for him, and the solace it had brought to him. For this reason, he considered it very important to pray for others, especially those in need of deliverance.

The volunteers readily provided a listening ear to anyone who needed a confidant. Most of the people who visited the centre needed someone in whom they could confide without the feeling of being judged. They appreciated the help they received, but more than that, they wanted their circumstances to change. Being aware that it took a power that they did not posses, many, despite their claim that they were not religious, frequently requested prayer.

Matthew's goal was to point people to the Source that had given him a second chance. Prayer provided the ideal opportunity. At the entrance of the centre, he placed a sign informing those visitors that there were volunteers ready to pray with anyone who requested it, and inviting individuals to place their prayer requests in the box located below the sign.

Those who desired prayer wrote their requests on numbered folding cards, allowing only the writer and the intercessor to see them. They would then meet and talk with their intercessor in a small room adjacent to the waiting room.

There, the intercessors laid out their prayer requests before the Lord. This intervention resulted not only in individual lives being changed, but in broken family relationships being mended and marriages reconciled. The results of Matthew's endeavor convinced him that he was fulfilling God's intended purpose for his life. This made him confident that God would also provide for all his other needs, and for those of his family.

Rebecca, on her part, fully regained her confidence, and once again saw her husband as an honorable man and herself a lovable person. The love and respect with which he now treated her, gave her a strong sense of security.

Although he had not yet found gainful, fulltime employment, she knew that all would be well. They had come to realize that, as the eyes of God were upon the smallest of His creatures, so too, He watched over them. Rebecca now felt confident enough to accept Leah's invitation, which resulted in a close and lasting friendship between them.

Little did Kezia know that her efforts to reach out to her lonely classmate would have paved the way of hope for the entire family and positively influence a whole community. Little did she know that Marissa, the pouting, people-repellant, who felt

AN ACT OF COMPASSION

no sense of belonging, who liked no one, and whom no one liked, would have blossomed into a delightful young woman who would gain great respect among her peer.

Even Marissa's teachers commented on the change in her personality, not to mention the improvement in her grades. Emerging from the lower end of her class, she now ranked among the top five academic achievers.

In addition, she joined the basketball team, took music lessons, and even joined a singing group that regularly visited elderly residents in a long-term care facility. Desiring to contribute to the wellbeing of the residents, she made beautiful personalized greeting cards, which brought sheer joy to all who received them. This ministry kept her very busy, but nothing gave her greater satisfaction than the happy faces of the appreciative recipients of her handiwork.

THIRTEEN
FAMILY REUNION

By this time, Chantelle had come to realize that she had been mistaken about Marissa. Marissa's talents, her skills, and her pleasing personality having surfaced, Chantelle now recognized her as a person of equal value as herself. She regretted the way she had treated Marissa and wanted to apologize, but did not know how.

Her opportunity came when Marissa scored the winning goal against their biggest basketball rival. That made a great impression on Chantelle. As they were leaving the field after the game, she walked up beside Marissa.

"Hi Marissa!" she smiled, a bit timidly.

At the sound of her name, Marissa looked around with a start. "Chantelle!" she exclaimed inwardly. That made her even more surprised. Chantelle had called her by name for the first time. What could this mean?

"Can I talk to you for a minute?" Chantelle asked, subdued.

"Sure", Marissa replied questioningly.

"I should have said this a long time ago".

"Said what?"

"Well, you know the way I have been treating you".

Marissa listened silently.

"Well, I now realize how unkind I have been to you", Chantelle swallowed. "I'm sorry".

Marissa recognized how much courage that took.

"Thank you for apologizing", she responded softly. "I know that was not easy. Don't worry, all is forgiven".

"All is forgiven? Really? I'm forgiven just like that? You mean you are not going to make me suffer even just a little?"

Marissa laughed. "Not at all! Why should I?"

"Well, because I gave you a rotten time, that's why!" Chantelle replied, almost indignantly.

"That's true. You did! However, Jesus says that if someone hurts us, and asks for forgiveness, we should readily forgive. You apologized. I accept that, and I forgive you", Marissa replied, maintaining her smile.

"You are not angry?"

"Not any more. I was very angry with you for a while, but when I learned about Jesus and I started to pray, I stopped hating you, although I did not trust you".

"I don't blame you", Chantelle replied remorsefully. "I know I caused you a lot of pain. Thank you for forgiving me so easily. Quite frankly, I don't deserve it", Chantelle said sheepishly.

"Well, that might be true, but God forgave me for all the rotten things I ever did, when I did not deserve it. He says I should do the same for others".

"I see".

"Come to think of it, I understand why you acted that way".

"You do?" Chantelle replied with a quizzical frown.

AN ACT OF COMPASSION

"Yes, in a way, I think I do. Do you remember that discussion we had in class about how most people tend to put their own feelings and needs above those of others?"

"Yes, I remember. Mrs. Goodman says it's human nature".

"That's true. When people smile at us, we feel as if they are saying, 'I think you're okay' or, 'I care about you'. When they don't, we think they are saying, 'You don't matter' or 'I don't like you'. That can result in an unfavorable reaction", Marissa explained.

"Yeah, you're right! I know exactly what you mean", Chantelle replied.

"Generally, people do not consider what might be happening with others to cause them to appear unfriendly", Marissa continued. "They either just stay away, or become antagonistic. However, if you think about it, happy people would be much happier if they shared their happiness, not only with those who are cheerful, but especially with those who are not. Doesn't it make you feel better when you make someone else smile?"

"You're right. It does!" Chantelle smiled. "You sound so grown-up!"

"I've been doing Bible study and I've learned a lot", Marissa replied.

"That's great!"

"Would you like to do Bible study, too? It will help you in everything you do in life".

"Thanks. I'll keep it in mind, but for now, I think I'll pass".

"Okay. Tell you what, Chantelle, let's erase our past experience with each other as if it never happened and start all over. Cool?"

"Cool!"

"Great! High five?" Marissa said, flashing Chantelle a broad, inviting smile.

"High five!" Chantelle echoed. "You did us real proud today, girlfriend", she added, as the two hands connected energetically. "You played a great game!"

"Thanks", Marissa replied modestly, "it was all team work".

"There's something I want to ask you",

Chantelle said, as they lowered their hands.

"Sure, ask away!"

"If I had not apologized, would you have forgiven me?"

"Good question. After I came to know about the love of Jesus, all the resentment I felt toward you disappeared. My heart became open to forgiving you, but until you apologized, I could not trust you or relate to you as if you had never hurt me".

"So when you forgive someone you treat them as you would if they had never hurt you?"

"That's the way I understand it".

"I see. I've heard people say that they have forgiven, but want nothing to do with those who hurt them".

"I know. I've heard that too, but when our Father in heaven forgives us, He restores us completely. He does not hold our past sins against us. He says we should forgive as He forgives".

"That's very interesting", Chantelle mused.

"We should never seek revenge or harbor hate toward those who offend us, but that is not the same as forgiving someone. Jesus says that if someone offends us and asks for forgiveness, we should forgive[1]".

"I think I heard something about Jesus forgiving the people who crucified him. *They* did not ask for forgiveness".

"That is true. Jesus made forgiveness available to them, by asking His Father to forgive them. However, if they did not accept that forgiveness, by confessing their sins and seeking forgiveness, they would not receive it. Otherwise, the people who crucified Jesus would be saved without repenting, and there is no salvation without repentance", Marissa explained.

"I see. You mean that when Jesus asked the Father to forgive those who did such horrible things to Him, they were still required to do their part in order to be saved?" Chantelle asked.

"That's right. In order for true forgiveness to occur, there must be repentance. As I understand it, repentance is to forgiveness as a key is to a lock. It is

---

[1] Luke 17: 3

true that saying you're sorry can be very difficult at times, but sometimes actions can be even more effective in showing remorse than words.

"I will give you an example. One day when I was about ten, my sister and I had a disagreement, and I was mad at her. She was baking a cake for dessert, and turned her back on the dry ingredients she had measured out.

"Then an idea came to me. I mixed in a tablespoon of salt. That will show her! I thought. She came back and continued her baking, having not a clue about the extra bit of flavouring.

"We had company that night, and everyone wanted to sample the cake, because it looked so delicious. One of our guests tasted it first and washed it down quickly with a big gulp of water, so as not to embarrass my mother.

"When Mom tasted it, she grabbed her serviette, so she could get it out of her mouth fast. At that, I ran from the table and burst out crying. My sister then figured out what had happened, and probably, so did everyone else.

"I got the courage much later to tell her that I was sorry, but she had already forgiven me, because, although I did not express it in words, she could see how sorry I was. I thought she would never have let me back in the kitchen when she was cooking, but she did. With God it's different, though, we have to confess our sins and ask for forgiveness, before we can receive it.

"Sometimes people do not realize that they have hurt us. In such cases, we need to express our feelings and give them an opportunity to make things right. If that is impossible, as in the case of someone moving away or passing away, our part is to make sure that we release them from any ill feeling that their actions may have evoked in us. We should never hate anyone or wish them harm".

"Okay. I have one more question for you".

"I'm listening", Marissa replied attentively.

"If it is the natural tendency of most people to shun those who seem unfriendly, why didn't Kezia treat you the way I did?"

"I'm glad you asked that question. Most people

follow their natural tendencies, but Kezia showed me kindness because she was a follower of Jesus Christ, as I have come to be. Jesus teaches that we should not judge, but that we should love everyone, even those who hate us or hurt us, and those who may be difficult for us to like.

"If we have good reason to believe that they intend to harm us, it would be wise to keep out of their way. Even so, we should love them and be ready to help them, when necessary. Kezia reached out to me because, with the love of Jesus in her heart, she could see beyond my appearance, and treated me as Jesus would", Marissa explained.

"That's amazing! Isn't that a hard thing to do? I mean, I can't imagine loving someone who hates me, and actually helping them!"

"In our own strength, it's not only hard, it's impossible. But when we depend on Jesus, He strengthens us to do what's right, however difficult it may be".

"I see", Chantelle replied contemplatively.

"Hey guys! Are you coming?" Kezia called,

interrupting their conversation, as she finished talking with Coach Donnelly.

"Okay, Marissa, we'd better get going", Chantelle urged. "All the showers in the locker room are probably taken by now, but I'm really glad we had this conversation".

"So am I!" Marissa replied, as they hurried off to join Kezia.

With much effort on Kezia's part, she and Chantelle had gradually rekindled their friendship. Over time, Chantelle had also become less hostile toward Marissa, as she noticed the change in her personality and that her refusal to speak to Marissa would not change Kezia's decision to befriend her.

Making things right with Marissa not only dissolved the tension between Chantelle and Kezia. It strengthened their friendship with each other and, in addition, gained Chantelle a new friend.

FOURTEEN
Onward and Upward

As Marissa and Chantelle approached her, Kezia asked with a curious smile, "What were you two talking about?"

"Oh, just stuff," Chantelle replied.

"Mm. Good stuff, I hope".

"Yeah, real good stuff", Marissa assured her.

"I got that feeling. You even seemed comfortable with each other. That's way cool!"

"Well, believe it or not, I made things right with Marissa!" Chantelle exclaimed.

"That's awesome!" Kezia returned, as she wrapped an arm around each of them. "I'm *so* glad!"

The three walked and talked together with Kezia in the middle until they came to the locker room. Back in the locker room, they chatted for a while longer, before starting out for home.

ONWARD AND UPWARD

On the way, Chantelle asked, "Kez, would you like to come over to my house on Sunday afternoon. We could study together for our biology exam, and just chill out a bit".

"You're on!"

"How about you, Marissa? Would you like to come?"

"I'd love to. Thank you!"

"It's a date then", Chantelle smiled, and then added, "I can't wait to get home. I'm beat".

"Yeah, I know the feeling", Marissa agreed.

"Tomorrow's Friday! Thank God!" Kezia exclaimed.

"Yeah, thank God", Marissa echoed.

"My sentiment exactly!" Chantelle joined in.

As the three girls started out for home, the screeching wheels of a car jolted them out of their conversation, as it pulled up to the curb alongside them.

"Hello, young ladies. Would anyone like a ride home?"

"Dad!" Kezia exclaimed, as all three turned their

heads together. "Great timing!"

"How cool is that!" Chantelle exclaimed, as they all climbed in.

"I sure was not looking forward to walking home", Kezia confessed. "Thank you Lord! Thank you Dad!"

As soon as they sat in the car they began to talk about how good it felt to have won the game.

"Marissa, you were awesome today!" Kezia commended her.

"That's because you're such a great team leader!" Marissa replied.

"No, really, you deserve all the credit. You saved the day. Dad, you should have seen Marissa on the field today. She played like a pro. Didn't she, Chantelle?"

"She sure did!"

"Oh, c'mon, you guys! It was no big deal", Marissa smiled, blushing mildly, but enjoying the attention.

"So you finally beat the Chipmunks, huh! Good for you!" Kezia's Dad gave them their well-deserved kudos.

"We sure did! We gave them a good whipping, too! We Nightingales don't play around, we just play", Kezia bragged.

"Congratulations! Good work, Marissa! You seem to have been the star of the game".

"Thank you, Dr. Lafontaine!" Marissa beamed.

A compliment from her classmates felt great. Getting one from Kezia's Dad boosted her confidence even more. It gave her an amazing sense of satisfaction.

Kezia had another reason to be happy. She was overjoyed at Chantelle's change of attitude toward Marissa, but Chantelle was not the only one who had a change of attitude. Marissa's classmates, who had never spoken to her before, complimented her on her performance. Some even invited her to weekend events, but spending Sunday afternoon studying with Kezia and Chantelle took priority.

Since they were both high achievers, with Kezia at the top of the class, she could not think of a better pair of study buddies. Besides, she had never before

AN ACT OF COMPASSION

spent time with both of them together in a friendly setting, and looked forward to that. In addition, she had received an invitation to attend a celebration at the home of the Kirkpatricks on Saturday night. She looked forward to that with great excitement.

Unfortunately, not everyone shared the excitement of Marissa's success, or her new image. Jealousy, being the enemy of prosperity, reared its ugly head, but unfriendly stares and derogatory comments did not faze her. She chose instead to give thanks to God for having brought her out of that horrible pit and set her feet upon a firm foundation. She also reminded herself of Psalm 119: 165, which says 'Great peace have they which love thy law and nothing shall offend them'. She called to mind a gem she had memorized in Proverbs 15: 1, which says, 'A gentle answer turns away wrath, but a harsh word stirs up anger[1]. With these treasures in her heart, she was able to return kind words when confronted with harsh ones. In so doing, she won the hearts of many of her antagonists.

---

[1] New International Version

ONWARD AND UPWARD

Despite the positive changes they had experienced, up until this point, the McBride's financial situation remained unchanged. The danger of losing their house still loomed menacingly over their heads. Marissa, now having grown in faith, trusted in God to bring about the desired solution. She called to mind frequently Philippians 4: 19, which says …'my God shall supply all your needs according to his riches in glory by Christ Jesus'. This enabled her to maintain an optimistic outlook, and to be happy in the face of all her challenges.

Despite the high she had experienced being the hero that got her team the envied trophy, the invitation to the Kirkpatrick's was the highlight of her week. She could not contain her excitement, as she waited for Saturday night to come. As did everyone else in her neighborhood, she had heard of the Kirkpatricks. Until recently, however, she was not aware that they were members of her church. She had started attending while they were away, and so had not had the opportunity to meet them. Now she would have the opportunity to go swimming in

AN ACT OF COMPASSION

the moonlight in their Olympic-sized swimming pool. That would be a new and exciting experience for her, and probably one that she would never forget.

Richard Kirkpatrick, who owned several healthcare centers in various locations, was also highly recognized for his charitable work in the community. He directed much of his interests toward youth development and also to services for the poor. His interest included funding recreational facilities, awarding scholarships, and giving food and clothing to those in need. His major goal was to provide wholesome choices aimed at shaping young minds into the responsible, productive human beings God intended them to be.

The Kirkpatricks and the Lafontaines were great friends. They played golf together and sometimes went camping together in the summertime. Marissa and her parents were delighted when Mrs. Lafontaine got them an invitation to the event. Having seen them on television many times in the past, Marissa could not help wondering what they would be like in person. The Lafontaines, meanwhile, knowing that Richard was looking for a managing director for one of his facilities, offered to introduce Matthew as a possible candidate for the job.

The Kirkpatricks had had a banner year thus far, and were celebrating their accomplishment. If, at the same time, they could find the right person for their newest addition, that would be the icing on the cake. The Lafontaines, on the other hand, knew that this could be a great opportunity for Matthew. Securing this position would enable the Mc Brides to pay their mortgage and save their home. It would be the ideal solution to their problem.

Matthew's experience as a business manager was limited to supervising his college campus bookstore as a student. However, being a quick study, he was sure he would have it down pat in no time flat. Why then was he so nervous, he wondered, as he prepared to go the event. He had understood from the Lafontaines that Richard Kirkpatrick was a very down-to-earth and humble man, who loved people,

AN ACT OF COMPASSION

and would go out of his way to help them. They had described him and his wife as friendly and easygoing, with a natural talent for putting people at ease. Matthew reminded himself frequently of that, but it did little to allay his anxieties.

He had never met anyone before, who knew the Kirkpatricks personally. Now he was invited to their home, where he was going to be interviewed for a position in their establishment. He felt honored, but not very confident. He really wanted this job. He wanted it badly. The prospect of returning to work excited him. He wanted nothing to interfere with his chances. He prayed that God would give him the confidence, the right attitude and the composure he needed to make a good first impression.

As he prepared, he remembered a text he had noted in Mark 11:24 during one of his morning devotions, which says, '…whatever you ask for in prayer, believe that you have received it, and it will be yours[1]'. He prayed that God would enable him to exercise the faith to believe he had actually received

---

[1] New International Version

that for which he had prayed.

It was hard at first for him to believe that he had received that which he had not seen, but as he kept repeating the text, he started believing that God had given him the job. He pictured himself in his office. He saw himself interacting with his staff. He imagined himself passing by clients as he walked down the hall, and exchanging a friendly greeting with them. He kept that text in mind constantly. As the evening wore on, his confidence became steadily stronger. He began to feel a calm settle over him. He would trust the Lord to work on his behalf, and leave the matter in His hands.

That was a wise decision. As it turned out, he needed not have worried. God had gone before him and prepared the way for him. When the time for his introduction finally came, he experienced no anxiety, only an inexplicable sense of calm. He felt more confident than he ever did before. With his gentle manner and quick-wittedness, he made a lasting first impression on the Kirkpatricks. He demonstrated all the qualities Richard wanted to see in the person he would hire. He saw in Matthew the integrity, the capability, the enthusiasm, the discipline and the caring nature that the position required. Matthew credited it all to the transformation that resulted from surrendering his life to Christ, and the guidance of the Holy Spirit.

Not only did he ace the interview, he entertained the Kirkpatricks and their guests with side-splitting jokes, making them laugh to the point of tears, and Richard challenging him to a game of table tennis. In that game, he scored more points, by proving himself a worthy opponent and a cheerful loser. They found that to be a winning combination.

Overall, the evening was very profitable, with Matthew taking home the grand prize. He got the job! He would be reporting for orientation on Wednesday. That was kind of short notice, but he had no complaints. His heart swelled with gratitude to God for opening up this wonderful door of opportunity for him.

Marissa, on her part, had an unforgettable experience. She had a chance to meet many prominent people, but her greatest excitement came when she had the opportunity to hang out with Lindsay—the Kirkpatricks' teen-aged daughter. She was a chip off the old block. Like her Dad, her warmth and friendliness put everyone at ease. At the end of the evening, they exchanged phone numbers and made plans to get together again soon.

Kezia and Lindsay had been friends since kindergarten. They had adopted each other as sisters, since neither of them had a sister. Now it seemed the family would expand with Marissa sharing their friendship. She had hit it off big with Lindsay, much to Kezia's delight. They looked forward to many more get-togethers in the future.

The day following the Kirkpatrick celebration, Kezia and Marissa went over to Chantelle's house to study, as planned, but it was difficult to concentrate. All they could think about was the great time they had spent at the Kirkpatricks'. Chantelle loved their beautiful house and their awesome furniture. Marissa was mostly impressed by their hospitality. She also found it fascinating that not only did they

AN ACT OF COMPASSION

share their wealth with the needy, but also their time, being heavily involved in charitable work.

In the past, they had served as missionaries to Fiji. In addition to their respective occupations, they now volunteered with a medical team, assisting people in different parts of the world, who could not afford medical treatment. Mrs. Kirkpatrick, herself a physician, also ran a non-profit organization for young single parents, providing counseling, and assisting them with their various needs. The support of dedicated staff and volunteers made it possible for her to readily respond whenever the call to foreign missions came. Lindsay had travelled with her parents on several mission trips. Marissa found that fascinating. She dreamed of some day becoming a missionary.

"All right guys, enough reminiscing. It's time to hit the books!" Kezia interrupted, jarring everyone back to reality.

"Yep! You're right. Unless we all want to see that sprawling red "F" from Mr. Grumble's eager pen decorating the front page of our exam paper, we'd better get cracking", Chantelle added.

"You're right!" Marissa agreed.

"Would you guys like a drink of juice or something before we begin?" Chantelle offered.

"Maybe later, thank you very much", Marissa declined gracefully, as did Kezia.

"Before we begin, let's ask the Lord to guide us and help us understand and remember what we are about to study", Kezia suggested.

"Oh, definitely!" Marissa said.

"We need all the help we can get!" Chantelle agreed.

With all heads bowed and eyes closed, Kezia prayed:

"Father in heaven, we know that all power is in Your hands, and that there is no request too big or too small for you to grant. Please help that our minds may be alert to grasp and to recall the information we are about to study, so that we may succeed in achieving the high scores on our exam that we desire. In the name of Jesus, we ask this. We thank You and we praise You in His name. Amen".

AN ACT OF COMPASSION

As soon as the prayer ended, Chantelle blurted out. "Guys, before we begin, I have a confession to make. I just feel an urge to do this".

"A confession?" Kezia and Marissa responded, simultaneously.

"Yeah, there is something I want you both to know. It came to me as you were praying, and I just have to say it".

"Okay, let's hear it", Kezia encouraged, as she and Marissa leaned forward attentively.

"Kezia", she began, "I know how pleased you are that Marissa and I are now on good terms, but I never apologized to you for the way I treated you when you first became friends with her. I was jealous of your friendship. I felt as if she was taking my place. I am so sorry. And, Marissa, as I told you, I am sorry that I jumped to the wrong conclusion about you, but now that I know you better, I think you're like, *way* cool!"

"Thank you!" Marissa smiled. "You're not so bad yourself, now that *I've* come to know *you* better".

"Thank you", Chantelle smiled.

"Thank you, Chantelle, for apologizing. I am just so glad you have come to see things differently", Kezia responded.

"Since it *is* confession time, I have one of my own", Marissa announced.

"We're all ears", Kezia and Chantelle responded in unison.

"Kezia, I am sorry for the way I acted toward you when we first met. I gave you a real hard time, when you were only trying to help".

"I understand. You were going through a lot. I'm just glad you *did* let me into your life, eventually. I mean, look what I would have missed!"

"And I am *so* glad you insisted on sticking your nose into my business!" Marissa laughed, joined by Kezia and Chantelle.

"It was my pleasure!" Kezia returned, followed by more laughter.

"I was very angry, but it did not take me long to see that you were sincere. Although I played tough, something about you appealed to me. You were just so annoyingly sweet! Actually, you brought me close to returning your smile at one point, but that would have blown my image and *I was just not going to give you that satisfaction!"* Marissa stated so comically Chantelle and Kezia could not help cracking up. "As for you, Chantelle, you thought that three would be a crowd, and you were right!"

"I was *right*?" Chantelle asked, puzzled.

"Oh, yeah! You were right! Three's a crowd, as we are now; but we are a happy crowd, aren't we?" Marissa smiled.

"We sure are!" Chantelle and Kezia again replied in unison.

"Group hug, anyone?" Kezia invited.

"I was just thinking the same thing!" Chantelle agreed, as they moved toward each other in a warm embrace.

"Now let's get down to business, shall we?" Kezia mimicked Mr. Grumble so closely, Marissa and Chantelle could not resist yet one more bout of laughter, before settling down to serious uninterrupted study. At the end of the session, they quizzed each other.

"What do you think?" Kezia asked. "Are we ready to take on Mr. Grumble?"

""We'll ace that test!" Marissa exclaimed. "It's a-piece-a-cake".

"Speaking of which, snack time, anyone?" Chantelle again offered.

"Yes, please!" Marissa and Kezia replied eagerly. By this time all three were famished.

"I'll be *right* back!" Chantelle lighted down the stairs to the kitchen, returning after a few minutes, with a tray full of goodies.

"By the way, Kez, there's something I've been meaning to ask you", Marissa said, helping herself to a bunch of grapes.

"Okay, ask away!"

"How did you come by the name Kezia? It's kind of unusual, isn't it?"

"I guess so. Funny you should ask, though. My Dad gave me that name", Kezia beamed. "It came from the Bible. Have you ever heard of Job?"

"I've heard a little about him. Grandma Beth

AN ACT OF COMPASSION

used to say her Dad had the patience of Job, because he allowed her in his workshop when she was little, and actually taught her stuff, even after she hit his thumb with a hammer while he was teaching her how to make a box for her toys. So I know that Job must have been a very patient man, but that's all I know about him".

"Well, that's true, he was very patient, but there's a lot more about him than that. Job was a righteous man, who was also very rich. He went through a great trial, during which he lost all that he had, even his children. It was very difficult, but through it all, he remained faithful to God. At the end of his trial, God gave him back twice as much as he had before. He also gave him back his seven sons and three daughters, the exact number of children he had before. He did not give him twice as many children as he had before, because the ones he lost during his trial will rise again in the resurrection when Jesus returns. So in the end, Job will still end up with twice his original number of children. Anyway, his new daughters were the three most beautiful girls in town. Well, Kezia was one of them.

"I thought that was very interesting when I heard it, but it gets even better. Mom's maiden name is Job. When she married Dad, she wanted to keep her family name, because she was an only child. Since I am also an only child, I have both my parent's family names. Dad named me Kezia because he had gone through a great trial himself, almost like Job's. When I was born, he thought of me as a gift from God, so he named me Kezia after one of Job's daughters. So, there you have it! I am Kezia Job-Lafontaine, at your service! Thank you for giving me the opportunity to tell my story. I think it's pretty neat, if I do say so myself".

"Wow! How cool is that! Do you know if your name has a meaning?" Marissa asked.

"As a matter of fact it does. Kezia means cassia—a sweet smelling spice".

"Awesome! That's a fitting name for someone like you".

"Thank you".

"I wonder if there's a meaning to *my* name".

"Meaning or no meaning", Chantelle reassured her, "you have a very impressive name, and it suits you well".

"Thank you, Chantelle! That's a lovely thing to say".

"Hey, I mean it. Ma-rissa McBride! That's a totally classy name".

"Why, thank you, Ma'am!" Marissa smiled, attempting a Victorian style curtsy, causing Kezia and Chantelle to burst out laughing.

At the end of the evening, the girls reflected on how far they had come. Chantelle had come to realize that things are not always the way they appear. She discovered that Marissa's hostile appearance was not a reflection of herself as a person, but of her inner turmoil. She had wrongfully judged Marissa as a bad person, and refused to associate with her, based on her own misguided perception. She came to realize how wrong she had been, and that she was in no way superior to Marissa.

In contrast, Kezia, instead of ostracizing Marissa,

as others did, had made an effort to connect with her. As a result, Marissa and her entire family came to know a better way of life. They became acquainted with Jesus Christ, who excludes no one, but gave His life for all. This act of compassion brought out the best in Marissa, likely saving her from a life of rejection and misery. Kezia knew that God alone knows the heart of man, and that a person's appearance does not determine a person's worth.

She carried as her motto the admonition of Jesus found in Matthew 7:12, universally known as the Golden Rule, which says, 'Do to others whatever you would like them to do to you...[1]'. She believed that by heeding this instruction, all conflicts could be averted, and that if everyone embraced this principle, peace would prevail.

In addition to the marked change that her intervention brought to Marissa and her family, that little seed bloomed and grew into a tree, producing an abundant harvest. It resulted in many accepting

---

[1] New Living Translation

the precious gift of salvation through Jesus Christ. Many who had already accepted that gift came to realize that the law of God stands forever and cannot be changed by man, and that what they thought was a commandment of God was in fact, a tradition of men.

Kezia's simple act also resulted in many relationships repaired and broken lives mended. Avoiding Marissa would have robbed her of the opportunity of discovering the precious gem hidden beneath the veneer of an unfriendly face. By reaching out in love, not only did she bring positive change to the lives of Marissa and her family, and many others, but also great enrichment to her own life.

Knowing that we *are* our brother's keepers, and that God desires that we bear one another's burdens, all who profess the name of Christ could learn a valuable lesson from Kezia's act of compassion. Happiness, like money, multiplies when dispersed. By lifting the spirits of others, we pave the way to experience the fullness of joy God desires for us.

www.ingramcontent.com/pod-product-compliance
Lightning Source LLC
Chambersburg PA
CBHW071237160426
43196CB00009B/1093